BEGIN AT THE LIGHTHOUSE – LA FAROLA

La Farola is easily accessed by bus (take the fabulously air–conditioned Circulo 2), by taxi, or even on foot.

La Farola

La Farola is one of Spain's oldest lighthouses. Designed by the army engineer Joaquín M Pery y Guzmán it dates from 1817 and replaced an earlier lighthouse built in 1724. In 1885 it was refurbished and a new lighting device was added in a 4 metre addition to the top of the building. It was damaged by an earthquake in 1898 and not completely repaired until 1913.

In 1909 it was enlarged to include living accommodation for the lighthouse keeper and his family. It was further damaged by artillery during the Spanish Civil War in the 1930s and had to be extensively repaired and refurbished in 1939. Its name is unusual – the expression "La Farola" usually refers to much smaller lighthouses.

 Stand at the lighthouse and look around. You will see to one side a wall with metal railings above.

Cross over to this, turn to the right, and follow the line of this wall away from the lighthouse along **Paseo de la Farola**. The inner–basin of the port of Malaga is on your left.

Although there has been a port at Malaga since Phoenician times (nearly 3000 years ago) it was only from the late sixteenth century that the modern port developed. The development of the east quay (upon which La Farola sits) dates from 1588, bringing to fruition plans produced by the Italian engineer, F. Bursoto. Subsequently, much silting of the harbour led to a need for much further dredging and re-engineering of the harbour during the eighteenth and nineteenth centuries (in particular, implementation of an expansion plan produced by R. Yague in 1876).

 After about 100 metres the vertical railings change to horizontal. This is a good point to stop and take stock of the view.

The view of Malaga from Paseo de la Farola

Looking from left to right you can see:
• The large container port and the Goliat cement silos.
• The dry dock and car ferry terminal (serving the Spanish enclave of Melilla in Morocco – from where on 17 July 1936 an army uprising led by General Francisco Franco was the starting point of the Spanish Civil War).

- **La Equitativa building** – look for a tall building with a 'spike' on top. This stands at the bottom of Malaga's main shopping street – the elegant Calle Marques de Larios.
- Malaga's cathedral – the **Cathedral de la Encarnacion** – famous for its single tower.
- The **Alcazaba** – a fortified Moorish palace on the lower slopes of the Monte de Malaga, the hill which rises steeply above the eastern edge of the city.
- The **Castillo del Gibralfaro** – a fortified Moorish stronghold at the top of the Monte de Malaga. Look for the flags flying from its top).

That Malaga has a busy working port will be evident. Apart from Barcelona it is the busiest port in Mediterranean Spain. Its cruise liner business is growing rapidly, following the recent addition of large new berths and a new passenger terminal. 2007 saw some 240 cruise boats visiting – bringing some 292,000 passengers. In May 2007 on just one day a record number of over 9000 cruise holiday-makers disembarked to explore the city: most, it appeared, without any map or guide!

 Continue to walk along Paseo de la Farola (walking directly inland towards the Monte de Malaga– do not veer off right along the Paseo Maritima, beach promenade). Take the right hand side of the road, away from the port redevelopment works on the left.

Redevelopment of the inner–basin of the port

2005 saw the demolition of a very large and unsightly warehouse building which had stood between the quay–side and the long line of trees behind (forming part of the **Paseo del Parque**). This has opened up fine new views both to and from the harbour, and was the first stage in the present comprehensive redevelopment of this inner side of the port.

A large yacht marina (for large yachts) is planned, as well as bars, restaurants and shops. There is also proposed an Antonio Banderas Theatre School – **Banderas** being locally born, and still closely connected to the city: returning annually to participate in the Semana Santa Easter week processions. There will also be an Oceanographic Institute, and the city's aquarium will be re–sited.

 As you walk along Paseo de la Farola, you will pass two attractive 19th century buildings – the **College of Advocates** and the **Office of the Naval Commander** – as well as a number of elegant government offices dating from 1934. These nestle beneath the high–rise apartment blocks – dating from the 1960/70s – which typify this lively district of 'Malagueta'.

On your left you will see the old port chapel – **Capilla de Puerto** – dating from 1732. Now sadly rather derelict, this was moved to its present position as recently as the 1970s. It is anticipated that it will be restored as part of the present port redevelopment.

Concise Early History of Malaga

- An urban settlement has existed on and around the base of the Monte de Malaga since at least 800 BC when the **Phoenicians** – sea–faring coastal traders from present day Lebanon – established a base here, amongst their many along the Mediterranean and North African coasts. Vestiges of their influence remain to this day. The style of the local fishing boats (best seen a short walk along the coast at Pedregalejo or El Palo) remains closely akin to those used by the Phoenician founders. As we shall see some archaeological evidence from this period remains within the city (for example, in the basement exhibition at the Picasso Museum).

- Phoenician governance was followed by that of Greeks (from the 6th century BC), **Carthaginians** (from the 4th century BC), **Romans** (from 206 BC until the early 5th century AD), **Vandals** and **Visogoths** (until the 8th century AD), and the **Islamic Moors** – who entered Malaga in 711 and remained for several centuries (during which period culture reached dizzying heights) until the **reconquest** of Spain in the late 15th century under **Ferdinand and Isabela**, and their re–introduction, in militant form, of Christianity. Malaga itself was reconquered, following a short siege, in 1487.

- In very approximate terms the Romans governed for 600 years, the Moors for 750 years, and some 500 years have elapsed following the Christian 'reconquest' of Malaga. Keep in mind, therefore, that Malaga is much older than 'Spain'; and that its historical links lie strongly with North Africa and not just with the rest of Spain and Europe.

Move further along the Paseo de la Farola and you will see, on your left, the (replica) **Santissima Trinidad**.

Santissima Trinidad

The most famous Spanish warship of her day, the Santissima Trinidad played a central role in two of **Nelson's** battles. With her four gun–decks mounting a total of 136 guns she was reputed to be the largest ship in the world – although this was a false claim – she was appreciably smaller than the French navy's three–deckers.

Built in Havana in 1769, to the designs of the Irish naval architect Matthew Mullan, the Trinidad was originally a standard three-decked battleship (ie a ship which lay 'in line of battle'), mounting 116 guns. However, in 1795, her forecastle was joined to her quarterdeck, and a light battery of eight–pounder guns was mounted, thus creating her distinctive 'four–decker' appearance. But although this change certainly made her look more impressive, it considerably worsened her sailing qualities and her stability, and she tended to be a liability, rather than an asset, in battle. She was even given the nick-name "el Ponderoso".

She formed an alluring potential 'trophy' in any battle and the British certainly made very determined attempts to capture her. At the **Battle of Cape St Vincent** (14 February 1797), where she was the flagship of the Spanish commander in chief, General José de Córdoba, she came under attack from at least five British battleships including, briefly, from Commodore Nelson himself in HMS Captain.

After a heroic defence, in which she was totally dismasted and suffered over three hundred casualties, she surrendered. But, before the British could take possession of her, the commander–in–chief, Admiral Sir John Jervis, was forced by the arrival of fresh Spanish ships to break off the action. The Trinidad's crew managed to rig jury masts (ie makeshift repaired masts) and bring the battered ship safely into Cádiz harbour, despite a gallant attempt to recapture her by the British frigate HMS Terpsichore under Captain Richard Bowen.

Eight years later, however, she was less fortunate. At the **Battle of Trafalgar** (21 October 1805), flying the flag of Rear Admiral Don Baltazar de Cisneros, she was once again set upon by a concentration of British ships and eventually surrendered to HMS Neptune, commanded by Nelson's close friend Captain Thomas Fremantle. HMS Prince took her in tow, but she had been so badly damaged that she sank in the great storm that followed.

Continue along the Paseo de la Farola until you arrive at a large roundabout dominated by a magnificent rubber tree.

To the left of this you will see three linked pedestrian crossings. Take these and you will arrive at the **Paseo del Parque**.

Paseo del Parque

This park was the idea of **Canovas del Castillo** – the Malaga – born politician who later became Prime Minister of Spain and whose statue can be seen just beyond and to the right of the rubber tree mentioned above. For more about the remarkable Canovas del Castillo – described by one historian as a 'squint–eyed schoolmaster from Malaga who looked like an unmade bed', see Part Two of this Guide.

hill upon which the Castillo del Gibralfaro sits, and where you are now standing would have been lower and under shallow water. As the harbour was dredged, the dredgings were laid out on the adjacent land – so that the edge of the deepened port moved seaward, and a substantial strip of reclaimed land resulted. It was upon this land that the Paseo del Parque, and the fine row of buildings along its immediate northern side were developed.

Work began on the Parque in 1897 – on land then recently reclaimed from the sea. During the 19th century the harbour had become badly silted and in the years following 1892 substantial dredging was undertaken. Until this time the sea-land divide was much closer to the town than now. The shore ran up close to the

The Parque was conceived from the first as a botanical garden, containing specimens from each of the several continents. It was renovated, at substantial expense, in 2006-7. The mature trees were thinned a little, the paths relaid and widened, and many new ornamental features added.

 Turn left and walk down the Paseo del Parque.

There are a variety of paths. The main route on the left is the quieter and shadier of the two main routes – but the one on the right affords better views of several buildings of interest.

As you walk along this right hand path you will see on your right, in sequence, the **Three Graces fountain**, the formal **Gardens of Pedro Luis Alonso**, **Malaga Town Hall** and the **Banco de Espana** building.

The Three Graces fountain – Las Tres Gracias

This – surely the most attractive fountain in Malaga – is the work of a French sculptor, Alphonse Durenne. It was originally sited in the Plaza de la Constitucion, later in the Plaza de la Marina, before arriving at its present all too easily over-looked position in the centre of the busy traffic roundabout at the end of Paseo del Parque.

Malaga Town Hall – Ayuntamiento

An elaborately decorated, vanilla and grey coloured, neo–baroque building dating from 1919. Its architects were Guerrero Strachan (of whose work in Malaga we shall see much more) and Manuel Rivero Vera. The very fine external decoration was the work of Francisco Palma. The building was repainted in 2006.

The Banco de Espana

This is a neo–classical building with a columned portico – resembling somewhat a Greco–Roman temple. In splendid contrast, though, is the art deco carved lettering bearing the name of the building. Dating from 1933–36, it was designed by Jose Yarnoz

After passing the Banco de Espana building take the pedestrian crossing to the right and cross to a building with a blue tiled roof. This houses the administrative offices of Malaga University (the **Rector's House**).

Rector's House – Malaga University

This was built in 1923 in Neo–Mudejar (ie Neo–Moorish) style, to a design by Teodora de Anasagasti. It was originally the City's central post office, becoming the University's main administration building in 1986. Look for the 'letter–box' motif displayed on some of its walls, bearing witness to its original use.

Walk up the steps and go inside this building. Once inside, turn immediately to the right, and go down a flight of stairs.

At the bottom of the stairs you will see preserved *in situ* a part of the old city wall, dating originally from pre–Moorish times, and maintained through till the reconquest at the end of the 15th century.

Return to the ground floor and on your right (in the centre of the entrance hall) you will see preserved – again

in situ – some remains of a Roman fish–salting works. The word Malaga is thought to come from the Phoenician word 'Malaka', meaning 'salted fish'.

Exit the University building, cross back over one pedestrian crossing, and turn right.

As you walk along you will see to the right, and nestling in the deep shade of (another) giant rubber tree, the former house of the head gardener of the Parque – the **Casita del Jardinero**: built in 1908, and now a Tourist Information Office.

The next building along is the old customs building – the **Aduana**. Remember that until this land was reclaimed in the late 19th century, the quay–side ran beside this building.

Just beyond the Aduana take the pedestrian crossing on the left, cross back to the Paseo del Parque, and walk to the right.

Soon on your left there is a children's playground – with a quite delightful bronze statue of a donkey.

A clear photo opportunity here if you are with children: but take care – the metal gets hot in the sun!

Just before the end of the Paseo del Parque take the

Customs House – Aduana

This four–storey building, of neo–classical design, was planned as early as 1788 but was not completed until 1829 – although an inscription on the north–westerly wall – only legible when brought into relief by the shadow of the evening sun – would suggest 1842. By the time of completion it was not much needed for its originally intended customs duties function, and was for a number of years used instead as a cigarette and cigar–making tobacco factory.

The building is presently being renovated to house Malaga's substantial collection of paintings – currently in storage – and will become its **Fine Art Museum**. The collection will be that which was housed in the present Picasso Museum before that collection was removed in 2003 to make way for the present Picasso exhibits. It will contain paintings and sculptures by artists such as Murillo, Zurbaran, Morales "the divine", Alfonso Cano, Ribera and Lucio Giordano.

pedestrian crossing to the right – towards the Malaga Palacio hotel – and then take the crossing to the left.

Pay attention to the little green man. Follow his loping

*gait – and be sure to note
how his pace speeds up
as the lights are about to
change!*

You are now at the **Plaza de
la Marina** (formerly – Acera
de la Marina).

There is here (on the right
hand side of the Plaza) a row

of fine buildings, dating from
1948–1960, and designed
by Juan Jauregui Briales
(who also designed, more
controversially, the Hotel
Malaga Palacio which you
have just passed, and the **La
Equitativa** building – ahead
of you and with the spike on
top).

The first of the buildings you
reach on the **Plaza de la
Marina** – the Diputacion
de Malaga – contains an art
gallery which is open to the
public.

The next building contains
a ticket office for Malaga's
main theatre – the Teatro
Cervantes – which we shall
see later.

Immediately in front of this
ticket office is a statue of
Hans Christian Andersen.

*Another clear photo
opportunity: but be sure not
to leave without spotting the
Ugly Duckling!*

Now take the down–ward
flight of steps just in front of
this statue, and at the bottom
turn sharp left.

This is Malaga's **Interactive
Musical Instruments
Museum.**

Interactive Musical Instruments Museum

Open Monday – Friday
10–14hr and 16–20 hrs; weekends
11–15 hrs and 16.30–20.30 hrs

This interactive museum displays
over 300 instruments around
the world collected by D Miguel
Angel Piedrola Orta.

On leaving this
museum walk ahead
and a little to the
left – into the underground
car park!

Hans Christian Andersen statue

This bronze statue, by Jose Maria
Cordoba was a gift from the
Danish Royal Family in 2005. It
commemorates Hans Christian
Andersen's visit to Malaga in
1862. Andersen was clearly much
taken by the city. We shall see
in Part Two of this Guide his
description of the peace and
serenity of Malaga's English
Cemetery.

If you now walk a few yards either to your left or to your right you will see:

- some remnants of the old city wall,
- part of the façade of a Moorish defensive tower, and
- part of the port quay–side dating from the seventeenth century.

All this was revealed when this car park was built in 1988 as a part of the wholesale (and not entirely successful) redevelopment, by the architect Manuel Sola Morales, of the central open space above. That area is shortly to be redeveloped again, to become the terminal for two metro lines presently being constructed – one from the northern suburbs, and one from the west of the city: with a further line, to be tunnelled under the Paseo del Parque, and ending at La Malagueta. The metro lines are scheduled to open in 2012.

 Now follow the pedestrian crossing across to the centre of the underground car park and return up to ground level via the spiral staircase which surrounds the fountain of the Plaza de la Marina.

At the top of these steps turn right and walk a few metres seaward in the direction of the tall stone columns (soon to be demolished as part of the current port redevelopment) at the port entrance.

When you reach the railings look down and to the right and you will see a bronze statue of a traditional Malagueno fish seller: **El Cenachero.**

Statue – El Cenachero

This was made by Jaime Pimental in 1968. The name refers to 'cenachos': the panniers carrying the fish, traditionally made from esparto grass.

Now look ahead into the port area. More or less straight ahead, through the port entrance, can be seen the very fine **Port Authority Building.**

Port Authority Building

This was built between 1932 and 1935. The floor plan is square, making it unclear in which direction, if at all, the building faces. There is a projected tetrastyle Doric portico supporting a balcony which opens onto the central spans of the main floor,

where pilasters alternate with the windows. The portico is topped, over the cornice, by a pediment containing a clock and the coats of arms of the Engineers Corp and of the city.

Now turn your gaze by 90 degrees to the right, and you will see a tall building with a spike on the top: **La Equitativa Building**.

Return to the opposite (city, rather than sea) side of the Plaza de la Marina and take the pedestrian crossing towards the Barclays Bank.

Look to the left and you will see a roundabout on which there is a statue depicting **Manuel Domingo Larios y Larios**, 2nd Marques de Larios.

La Equitativa building

This building occupies the site of the former **Casa Larios**, whose owner, the 19th century industrialist, the **Marques de Larios**, was an important patron of the city – see immediately below.

The present building was built to a design by Juan Jauregui Briales in 1956, and is modelled – in miniature – on American skyscrapers. At first glance somewhat unprepossessing it is a building for which fondness grows over the time; and whose renovation seems somewhat overdue.

The Statue of Larios

This statue dating from 1899 and made of bronze on a marble pedestal was designed by Mariano Benilliure and celebrates Manuel Domingo Larios y Larios, 2nd Marques de Larios. The Larios family came originally from the La Rioja region of Spain, where they were cattle breeders. Following arrival in Malaga in the early nineteenth century they developed successful businesses processing

sugar cane, and in the tobacco and textile industries. The product with which their name is now most closely connected – Larios Gin – is, however, a connection which dates only from the early 1930s.

Larios was instrumental in securing the development of the Calle Marques de Larios, Malaga's finest shopping street, which runs immediately north from the statue.

The Marques is depicted standing on a grand pedestal, flanked by the figure of a man with a pickaxe and a shovel, representing labour, and a half–naked women who is offering a child to the Marques, and representing the gratitude of the city.

You are now at the junction between the **Alameda** – with its very fine avenue of mature shady plane and rubber trees, and **Calle Marques de Larios** – with its equally fine avenue of tempting shops.

Leave 'retail therapy' for a while and take the **Alameda**.

Walk along its right hand side, noting its beautifully ornate street lamps.

At the end of the first block there is a narrow alley–way to the right (just beyond Vodaphone). This alley is something of a local favourite – being home to a row of popular simple fish restaurants.

Continue along the Alameda. At the next intersection you are confronted by pedestrian barriers and so you will need to turn right for a few yards before taking the crossing and then returning to the Alameda. A consolation, as you take the crossing, is the view you get of the elaborate doorway to the very fine **Edificio Edipsa**.

Continue to the right along the Alameda until you see an alley on the right – Calle Pastora. On the corner of the Alameda

The Alameda

The Alameda was developed by Lopez Mercader in the years following 1783 when this area was reclaimed from the sea. In the 19th century it was known as the Salon de Bilboa. There was originally a central pedestrian walkway containing many sculptures and fountains, and carriageways on each side. Before the opening of Calle Marques de Larios at the end of the 19th century it was the finest street in Malaga and the hub of social life. It was bounded at the eastern end by Casa Larios, and there was at first no bridge across the river at the far western end. The central walkway was opened to traffic in 1925.

immediately ahead you will see some old wooden doors.

This is the former **Police Gaol – the Casa del Guardia**, which you should enter.

Old Police Gaol – Casa de Guardia

This bar has been serving the local wines from barrels since 1840 and is said to be the oldest surviving bar in the city. Order drinks by pointing to any of the barrels on the wall, and a record of what you drink will be chalked on the wooden counter in front of you.

These sweet wines are made from grape varieties such as Pedro Ximenes, Moscatel de Alejandria and Moscatel Morisco; and the results – **'Malaga dulces'** – are known by names such as Pajarete, Guinda, Solera, Moscatel Dorado Malaga Virgen, Quitapenas and Campanas.

 On 'Getting out of Gaol', turn right, and continue along the Alameda.

Note on your left, brightening the central reservation of the Alameda, the wonderfully colourful flower stalls.

Continue along the Alameda until you come to a bridge spanning the **Rio Guadalmedina**.

Not very exciting – the river is culverted at this point, although we shall see it re–surface a little later in the walk. What you see here is essentially a storm–water overflow.

Maybe it looked better in the nineteenth century?

Just beyond the far end of the bridge upon which you are standing is **El Corte Ingles** – Spain's leading department store.

But assuming you don't yet want to shop ….

Don't cross the river: but take the pedestrian crossing across the road (towards the rather interestingly designed **BBVA** building: noting its unusual horizontally sliding shutters).

Follow the line of the river down its 'left bank'.

In front of you in 200–300 metres there is a white–walled building, with, on its front, and in rather tiny letters, **CAC Malaga**. This is the, quite new, Museum of Contemporary Art.

CAC Malaga –
Contemporary Art Centre

Closed Mondays: Open Tues– Sat 10 – 20 hrs
Sun 10 – 14 hrs.

This opened in February 2003. The building was formerly a market – the Mercado Mayor. It comprises both a permanent collection and temporary exhibitions.

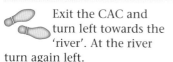

Exit the CAC and turn left towards the 'river'. At the river turn again left.

At about here the culverted water does at last emerge, with some gushing force.

Follow down the side of the river, with the CAC to your left. Note the former loading bays from when the CAC was a market hall.

Pass under a row of shady trees, and watch for birds skimming the surface of the river water: at last a proper river!

Just before the next river bridge take the pedestrian crossing to the left; and then

Aula de Mar – Aquarium

Open Monday – Friday
10 – 14.30.

A small aquarium, but with a wide variety of fish and some remarkably large turtles. It is well worth a visit, though, simply for its collection of wooden model sailing ships.

take the pedestrian crossing across the main road ahead. Beside this main road are two old cement–rendered port buildings, the second of which – notwithstanding some shabbiness – has some pretension to 'art deco' style.

Inside this second building is the **Malaga Aquarium** – the **Aula de Mar**.

On exiting the aquarium, turn right. After a few yards cross the busy road at the pedestrian crossing, and continue right along this main road – the **Avenida de M Agustin Heredia** – named after another of Malaga's principal industrialist benefactors.

Ahead, in the middle of the avenue, is a **bronze statue of Heredia**, looking a little forlorn, perhaps pondering Larios' rather more prominent position.

Continue along, not overlooking on the left a modern,18 storey, apartment block with interestingly ornamented concrete balconies.

As you walk further along the Avenida there is a row of shady cafes nestling in the shade of trees.

Number 16 is a notably attractive governmental building.

Shortly after, there is – also on the left – a quite charming small formal public garden.

Explore this, but be sure to note at the far end – as you leave the garden – the fattest and spikiest little tree you will surely ever see: looking up, its bark resembles a crocodile's thorny skin.

On leaving these gardens take the pedestrian crossing ahead, and then take a turn left towards a Barclays Bank.

Walk along under a row of ferny trees, and at the end of the block turn left, along what you may recognise as the south side of the Alameda.

Pass alongside numerous bus stops, and be sure to notice the attractive wrought iron–work ornamenting the lottery sellers' kiosks.

Watch out on the left for the doorway of the **Archivo Municipal** – the Municipal Archive.

On exiting, turn to the left and take the first pedestrian crossing (actually three linked crossings) back across to the other side of the Alameda – enjoying, in summer, the welcome depth of the shade cast by the avenue of trees.

At the end of the crossings follow a sign for **Atarazanas Market**, which you will see straight ahead.

Municipal Archive – Archivo Municipal

Make a point of at least glimpsing the inside of this fine building, which dates from 1792, and is one of the oldest buildings in the Alameda. The building was redesigned by Guerrero Strachan at the end of the 19th century. The City Council completely restored this building in the years immediately after 1985. There are usually public exhibitions of painting in the galleries within.

Atarazanas Market

The arched stone doorway to this building dates back to the 14th century, being built during Moorish rule. The word 'atarazanas' appears (depending on who you believe) to refer either to the former use of the building as a military arsenal, or (more probably) to its use as a workshop for boat building and repair, and rope–making. The latter is given further plausibility by the fact that in Moorish times, and indeed until the end of the 18th century, the sea came up close to this building.

In the late 1700s the building housed the Artillery Barracks,

and the College of Surgeons and was used as a hospital during epidemics.

In 1868 all was demolished except the arched stone doorway. Surrounding the stone entrance, the present iron structure was built in 1879, designed by Joaquin de Rucoba and Octavio de Toledo. It was Malaga's main fruit, vegetables, meat and fish market until new premises nearby were constructed in 2008.

The Atarazanas building is undergoing extensive renovation in 2008/9.

 Cross over to the building and walk around it to the right.

Turn right onto Calle Sagasta, noting the highly decorative, and rather unusual, Angules de Aquinada building.

On your left as you go down Calle Sagasta is the former **Felix Saenz** department store building, now under conversion to apartments.

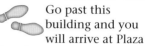 Go past this building and you will arrive at Plaza de Felix Saenz (named after Felix Saenz Calvo, the founder of the department-store who – like Heredia and Larios – made his fortune in Malaga having moved here from La Rioja).

Turn left, in the direction (in the distance) of a grey/white brick towered church: the **Iglesia de San Juan**.

Former Felix Saenz Department store building

This dates from 1912–14 and is in modernist style, with baroque elements. Its architect – depending on your source – was either Guerrero Strachan or Manuel Rivera Vera: perhaps it was both.

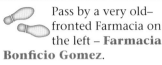 Pass by a very old–fronted Farmacia on the left – **Farmacia Bonficio Gomez**.

A little further along is the **Iglesia de San Juan**.

Walk along, keeping this church on your right. Follow the narrow alley, and turn left at the next junction – along Calle Cisneros.

Along this street you will see several flamenco costume shops: evidence that flamenco traditions remain very much alive.

At the end of Calle Cisneros you will see a bridge ahead over the river.

Stand on this bridge and look downstream. The next bridge you see – ignore a rather misleading local sign suggesting otherwise –is the so–called **German Bridge**, the **Puente de los Alemanas**.

The German Bridge – Puente de los Alemanas

An earlier bridge was washed away by floods which hit the city in 1907, and this replacement iron bridge was financed by the German Government in gratitude for the heroism of the people of Malaga in saving many German lives a few years earlier when the frigate **Gneisenau** became shipwrecked at the mouth of Malaga harbour in 1900.

The story of the wreck of the Gneisenau and the flood of 1907 is told in Part Two of this Guide.

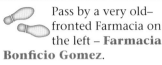 Do not cross the bridge you are standing on. Continue instead about 50 metres down the left bank of the river.

On your left look out for a small, old, building nestling beneath much large–scale building work. This is the delightful **Folklore and Costume Museum**.

Folklore and Costume Museum – Museo de Artes y Costumbres Populares

Closed Sundays
Open – Winter: 10–13.30 and 16–19 hrs
Summer: 10–13.30 and 17–20 hrs

This lovely museum is sited within the exquisite **Meson de la Victoria**, built in 1632 by monks from the Convent of La Victoria. It is of a design typical of inns dating from the 17th century.

Upstairs there is a fine collection of colourful posters advertising Malaga's annual *feria* (summer fiesta).

The collection of colourfully painted ceramic figures is also recommended. These depict the customs and traditions of Malaga in the 18th and 19th centuries.

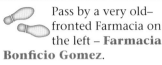 Exit the museum and turn left, and after just a few metres turn left again, down Calle de Acujero.

Immediately on your left you will see a building resembling

a large cage: is this a new 'supermarket–trolley' school of architecture?

This is the new Atarazanas market – and it is well worth a few minutes exploration inside.

Be sure to exit the way you entered, and turn left to walk further down Calle de Acujero.

You will see (again) at the end of this street the rear of the former **Atarazanas Market** (currently under renovation) – with its magnificent stained–glass window, depicting Malaga as viewed by ships arriving in the port.

As you walk toward the Market, don't miss the ornamentation on the balconies of the buildings on the left.

When you reach the former Atarazanas Market turn left.

In a few metres take Calle Herreria de Rey, and walk along beside the several buildings housing **Café Aranda** – a real city institution: where Malaguenos go for their morning (and afternoon) *churros con chocolate*. Marvel as you pass at the pouring skills of the waiters.

At the end of Calle Herreria de Rey walk straight across the small square and join Calle Alercon Lujan. Follow this until it connects with **Calle Marques de Larios**.

Calle Marques de Larios

This elegant street was completed in 1891, the culmination of a plan drawn up originally as far back as 1858. Initial work on the plan stalled, and real progress was made only once the industrialist, the Marques de Larios, took charge in 1886. Its principal architect was, once again, Strachan. The intention behind its construction was to link the city to the port area, by adding an exit to the Plaza de la Constitucion.

Extensively damaged by fire in the Civil War. it was subsequently rebuilt/restored in its original style. It was pedestrianised in 2003.

Turn left up Calle Marques de Larios and continue until it joins the **Plaza de la Constitucion**.

Plaza de la Constitucion
1998 Stengel & Co., Dresden 29746

Malaga

Plaza de la Constitucion – Constitution Square

This square, called **Plaza de la Constitucion** since 1812 – formerly **Plaza Major** and **Plaza de las Cuatro Calles** – has been at the heart of the city's life since the 15th century: hosting fiestas, bullfights, executions, and religious celebrations. Even today it hosts, almost weekly, some public event.

Walk diagonally to the middle of the square and you will see the **Genoa fountain**.

**The Genoa Fountain –
Fuerte de Genova/Fuerte de
Carlos V**

This ornamental fountain dates
from the 16th century, and is
regarded as a fine example of
Italian renaissance design. It is
decorated with aquatic motifs,
nymphs and children with
dolphins.

Continue across the
square diagonally,
and enter the
narrow **Calle Compania**.

The building at the junction
between Calle Compania and
the Plaza de la Constitucion
is that of the **Sociedad
Economica de Amigos del
Pais**.

Proceed down Calle
Compania and after
a few yards you will
see on the right a building
currently under renovation
– the 16th century **Palacio
Villalon**.

This will house (from late
2009/early 2010) part of the
art collection of **Baroness
Carmen Thyssen–
Bornemisza**. The collection

will comprise principally
Andalusian and other
Spanish art from the 19th
century.

Return to Plaza de la
Constitucion, and find
directly opposite the **Café
Central**.

Go inside and you will see
around the walls a large
number of old photographs
of this square. Note the
changes, decade by decade:
and devotees of "Where's
Wally" can have some
fun playing "Where's the
Parachutist".

Note also the tiled mural
displaying the different
names Malaguenos give to
different strengths of coffee.

Leave Café Central by the
doorway through which you
entered and go back out to
Plaza de la Constitucion.

Turn immediately left
and after just a few yards

Sociedad Economica de Amigos del Pais

Built in 1785, this is typical of 18th century
domestic architecture with continuous
balconies along the upper floors. Its most
significant element is its majestic portico of
veined marble. It was once the office of the
maritime consul and was later a Jesuit School.

You will see in due course a sign showing "Banos Arabes" – Arab baths: certainly worth a visit, but of quite modern origin.

Continue along Calle Granada.

A little further along, on the right, is the **Iglesia Santiago**.

turn left again to leave the Plaza de la Constitucion through the arched entrance to what was formerly a convent building. This alley is the **Pasaje Chinitas**.

Iglesia Santiago

This is the oldest of Malaga's churches, built on the site of a former mosque.

Note the square brick mudejar ('moorish') style tower, the pointed arch to a former entrance, and the white painted walls through which can be seen glimpses of the former decorated motifs.

It was here that **Picasso** was christened on 10th November 1881.

Turn down the first narrow alley on the left, and go straight over the next intersection of alleys.

On your right look out for Number 6 – surely one of Malaga's most 'Moorishly' ornamented private buildings.

Continue along until you come to an intersection – the **Plaza del Carbon** – with the Café Madrid opposite.

Take the pedestrianised road to the right – **Calle Granada**, and follow its snaking route for several minutes. This is one of the oldest streets in Malaga, forming the route down which Ferdinand and Isabela entered the city at the reconquest.

Be careful that you keep along this street, and do not inadvertently fork off into another.

Continue along Calle Granada and you will see ahead the **Plaza Merced**.

Plaza Merced – Our Lady of Mercy Square

According to excavations this appears long ago to have been the site of a Roman amphitheatre.

From the time of a Royal Decree in 1489 this area, just outside the former city walls, was home to a tax free market.

In due course there emerged around the square three convents. Immediately opposite from where you are standing was the **Convent La Paz** (1519 – mid 19th century); to the far left was the **Convent La Merced** (demolished in 1899); and on the right was the **Convent Santa Ana** (demolished in the early years of last century to make way for the **Victoria Eugenia cinema** – designed by Strachan, and dating from 1913). The side of the square on which you have joined Plaza Merced follows the line of the northern edge of the walls of the old Muslim city.

For much of the 19th century the square was known as '**Plaza Riego**' (after a liberal revolutionary, who led a military uprising in Cadiz in 1820).

The square was landscaped in pretty much its present form in the 18th century and most of the present buildings emerged in the mid/late 19th century. The iron for the railings within and around the square came from the Heredia factory, named after one of Malaga's leading industrialists and benefactors (whose statue we saw earlier on this walk).

In the centre is the **Torrijos obelisk** – of which, more later.

We shall return to this Plaza shortly, but for the moment turn left and walk along the south side of the square, exiting along Calle Alamos.

A few yards along on the left – at number 32 – is the **Doll's House Museum**.

Watch out for the rather charming sign projecting – just above Spanish head height – over the pavement.

Doll's House Museum – Museo de Munecas

Open Tues – Sun 11–13.00

This museum is housed in a restored 18th century baroque building. The collection has over 50 hand–made items dating back to 1850. Opening hours are not generous – but exhibits can sometimes be seen through the windows even when closed.

Exit the Doll's House Museum and turn to the left.

A block or two along, on the right at number 7, will be found the recently opened **Museo de Reales Oficios** – in the late 18th century **Palacio de los Marqueses de Cropani**.

Palacio de los Marqueses de Cropani: Textiles Museum

Open 11–14 hrs.

This is a 'must' to visit if only in order to enjoy the beautifully restored interior of this building.

 Exit and turn left, retracing your steps along Calle Alamos.

Quite soon turn left into Calle Carcer.

Walk up to the **Teatro Cervantes**.

Teatro Cervantes

This dates from 1870 and was built by Ramos Marin to a design by Jeronimo Cuervo.

It stands on the site of part of the former **Convent La Merced**, and replaced an earlier theatre which was destroyed by fire. Indeed, this replacement also suffered a fire not long before its opening.

Following a period during which the building suffered neglect, the city council acquired the property in 1984 and financed the works to renovate the building.

The renovated theatre, with a capacity of 1,171 seats – and excellent air–conditioning – was opened by Her Majesty Queen Sofía on 6th April 1987.

The ornately painted ceiling of the auditorium is by Bernardo Ferrandiz and Munoz Degrain. It depicts scenes typical of life in Malaga.

 Pass the Teatro Cervantes on its right hand side and visit the market – the **Mercado La Merced**.

Enter via the Supersol supermarket. Go down the steps into Supersol and take the exit immediately to the right into the market.

Explore the market and exit through its the bustling market café.

Go down the steps immediately outside the market café and cross the pedestrian crossing.

Immediately ahead, on the corner, is the **Picasso Birthplace Museum**.

Picasso Birthplace Museum

Open every day: 9.30–20 hrs

This building, on the site of the former convent de Santa Maria de la Paz dates from 1861 and was designed by Diego Clavero. It forms part of a block which runs along the north side of the Plaza Merced. This is collectively known as the Casas de Campos (completed in 1874) Its developer was Antonio Campos Galin, the Marques de Iznate; and its architect was Jeronimo Cuervas.

Picasso was born here on 25th

October, 1881. His father, Jose Ruiz Blasco (the "Picasso" side of the family was his mother's), was a painter and art teacher. In 1884 the Picasso family moved along the square to the 3rd floor of what is now number 17 (above the present Celtic Druid Irish Bar). The family left Malaga in April 1891 when Jose Ruiz Blasco was appointed to an art teaching position in La Coruna in northern Spain.

The museum comprises art galleries on the ground and first floors, together with an interesting first floor room which has been furnished and decorated in a style typical of Malaga in the late 19th century.

 On exiting the Picasso Birthplace Museum walk diagonally across the Plaza Merced. If it is early summer the jacaranda trees will be in magnificent full flower.

Look to your right, and see – above number 14 – a tiled mural depicting the former **Convent de la Merced**.

At number 13 there is a free–entry art gallery – run by the **Picasso Foundation**.

Note also the very fine upper window casings at number

12, and the undulating roof and guttering of numbers 9 and 10.

Half way across the Plaza Merced is the **Torrijos obelisk**.

The Torrijos obelisk

Following an unsuccessful uprising against the despotic King Ferdinand VII, **General Torrijos** was shot on December 11, 1831, along with around fifty of his supporters on the beach at San Andres, on the western side of the modern port area.

This memorial, designed by Rafael Mitjana, was constructed in 1842. The remains of Torrijos and his followers were moved to the completed monument on Sunday 11 December 1842 – and on the morning of that date each year the Torrijos Society hold beside the memorial a ceremony of remembrance.

It was renovated in 2006–7: when, slightly annoyingly, the upper sections of the column were put back not quite in alignment.

For the story of General Torrijos, see Part Two of this Guide.

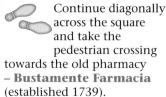 Continue diagonally across the square and take the pedestrian crossing towards the old pharmacy – **Bustamente Farmacia** (established 1739).

At the end of the crossing, turn left and walk in the direction of the road tunnel under the Monte de Malaga.

Turn first right down Calle Alcazabilla

In front of you, on the left, note the ornate "**Albeniz**" cinema – built in 1945, its future was quite recently made secure by action of the City Council.

Just before you reach the cinema, turn right into Calle Santiago.

At the end of Calle Santiago turn left.

A little further on turn left again into Calle San Agustin.

On your left is the **Picasso Museum**.

Picasso Museum

Closed Mondays. Open Tues – Thurs 10–20hrs, Fri and Sat 10–21 hrs, Sun 10–20 hrs.

The **Picasso Collection** is housed here in the former **Palacio de Buenavista**, a 16th century renaissance–style building, well worth a visit in its own right.

The Picasso Collection contains some 133 items donated by the artist's daughter in law, Christine: 14 paintings, 9 sculptures, 80 drawings, 58 engravings and 7 ceramic items; as well as 22 pieces donated by his grandson, Bernard.

Be sure to visit also the **archaeological museum** – somewhat hidden away in the basement – where some of the earliest, Phoenician, foundations of the city may be seen in situ. The discovery of these foundations caused some delay to the renovation of the building, and its reopening in October 2003 with the Picasso collection.

 On exiting the Picasso Museum turn left.

On your left – behind a flourishing bougainvillea – is the 'custard and maroon' exteriored, **Iglesia San Agustin**.

Continue straight on and you will see Malaga's magnificent **Cathedral de la Encarnacion**.

Malaga Cathedral: Cathedral de la Encarnacion

The **Cathedral de la Encarnacion** is built on the site of the city's former main mosque, the Aljama Mosque: which itself had been built on the site of a former Christian basilica.

Reconsecration occurred soon after the reconquista of 1487, the former mosque building sufficing initially for such Christian worship.

An initial project for a new building was started in the early 16th century – but abandoned as early as 1525 as being excessively costly.

The following year the most important Spanish architect of his day, Diego de Siloe, was commissioned to produce plans for a cathedral 'in renaissance style', and work began in 1527.

Work progressed quite well until the late 1580s, at which time there had been constructed the chancel and crossing (i.e. the eastern end of the cathedral – to your left from where you are standing). At this point religious services transferred from the old mosque to the new building.

Little further building took place for over a hundred years, until a survey in the early years of the 18th century indicated a real risk that what had been built might collapse unless the remainder was completed.

The remaining work was done to a new plan, devised by architect Jose de Bada y Navajas. Funds were obtained by way of inauguration of a new tax – the so–called Sisa Mayor – levied (at least in theory) on all cargoes of wine, raisins and olive oil shipped out of the city's port.

The new building and old were joined in 1764, but major construction work stopped in 1782 – leaving unbuilt the top part of the main facade and and the south tower. Hence the cathedral's nickname – **La Manquita** – the 'little one armed lady'.

A variety of explanations – of varying degrees of plausibility – exist for the work stopping in 1782. Amongst these are that:

- In 1780 the incumbent bishop, Miguel Murguiro, gave the necessary funds (400,000 Reales) to the American colonies

the Cathedral through the ticket–office.

Immediately ahead, in the centre of the cathedral are:

- Two 18th century **organs** – containing over 4000 pipes.
- Two rows of elaborately carved **choir stalls**. These contain some 42 sculptures carved by Pedro de Mana, Luiz Ortiz de Vargas and Jose Micael Alfero.

Walk around the interior of the cathedral, keeping the exterior wall on your left.

to help in their struggle for independence from Britain; and in particular to provide support to the Malagueno, Bernardo de Galvez, Governor of Louisiana (and subsequent founder of Galveston, Texas);

- The money was used as disaster relief following an earthquake in Mobile, Alabama – the site of one of Galvez' key battles in the war of independence and a city which retains a connection with Malaga through a 'twinning' link;
- The money was given to help fund the building of a church in Latin America;
- The decree, under which taxes had been levied to cover building costs, was revoked – perhaps in despair at the time being taken in completing the construction.

The very fine **Puerta de la Cadenas** (the so–called '**chain door**' – for reasons not entirely apparent) is straight ahead.

The **Visita Turistica** entrance is through a rounded arched doorway into a courtyard to the right of the Puerta de la Cadenas

Go through that this arched doorway and enter

The following side chapels are of most interest:

- **Capilla de la Encarnacion: No 21.** This contains a fine 18th century sculpture by Juan de Salazar – the Annunciation: the two figures immediately above the altar.
- **Capilla de Santa Barbara: No 20.** This contains the only altar–piece preserved from the old mosque cathedral.
- **Chapel of the Virgin of the Kings: No 18.** Give the painting in this chapel a 'miss' if you are squeamish.
- **Capilla de la Conception: No 11.** This chapel contains the fine 17th century painting, la Inmaculada (by Claudio Coello)
- **Chapel of our Lady of the Rosary: No 10.** The 17th century painting by Alonso Ceno is must-see for devotees of flying cherubs
- **Chapel of the Fallen: No 8.** A chapel to which the remains of Nationalist civil war dead were brought by their relatives for burial in the crypt below.

Exit the Cathedral by the same (from this direction half–hidden) entrance as you entered.

Turn left and walk through the delightfully shady cathedral gardens.

On the left, on the cathedral wall, look out for a plaque presented in 1997 by the (US) National Society for the American Revolution: giving credence to the first of the explanations (above) for the absence of funds to complete the cathedral.

Exit the gardens down some steps and then walk to the left nearly all the way around the exterior of the cathedral, keeping the building always on you left.

In just a few yards you will enter the **Plaza del Obispo**, containing an ornate **water fountain** and the **Episcopal Palace.** This is a good place to admire the cathedral's massive and contrastingly–marbled west front.

Episcopal Palace – Palacio Obispo

Closed Mondays, otherwise open 10–14hrs and 18–21 hrs.

This example of domestic baroque architecture dates from c 1800 and was designed by Antonio Ramos. It has a very fine entrance façade in pink, white and grey marble – reflecting similar colours on the western façade of the Cathedral.

A brief stroll inside the building is strongly recommended. There are generally exhibitions of art on display.

Water Fountain

This was constructed in 1785, the water coming into Malaga from the **aquaducto de San Telmo** a little to the north of the city

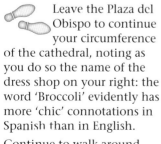

Leave the Plaza del Obispo to continue your circumference of the cathedral, noting as you do so the name of the dress shop on your right: the word 'Broccoli' evidently has more 'chic' connotations in Spanish than in English.

Continue to walk around the outside of the Cathedral,

noting that the south and east sides are much less ornate than the others.

On the far side of the cathedral, beside some formal gardens, you will see the elegant interiored **Café– Restaurant El Jardin**.

After passing the Cafe El Jardin turn to the right, along Calle Cister.

A little way along Calle Cister, on your left, is the small, but charming, **Museo de Arte Sacro**.

Continue to the end of Calle Cister, then bear very slightly to the left, and walk up a short stone–stepped slope to where can be viewed the **Roman Theatre**, and the entrance to the Moorish palace – the **Alcazaba**.

Roman Theatre – Teatro Romana

This was rediscovered as recently as June 1951, and somewhat problematically, during works to build a garden at the entrance to the **Palacio de Archivos Biblioteca y Museo** – itself in the course of construction. Notwithstanding this 'find', work on the Palacio continued, completing in 1956.

There then followed decades of debate, until the Palacio was demolished in the 1990s in order to allow full exploration of the site. Excavation is continuing apace, restoring to view the ever–more extensive remains.

The theatre dates from time of **Augustus** in the first century AD, and was used until the 3rd century.

Much stone from the theatre was later used as a source of building materials for the **Alcazaba** above. Notice, shortly, when within the Alcazaba, the roman marble columns and capitals incorporated into that later building, and the use of stones carved with Latin inscriptions.

Alcazaba

Closed Mondays, otherwise open in summer 9.30–20 hrs and winter from 8.30–19 hrs.

This beautiful palace–cum–hill–fortress was built mostly in the second half of the 11th century by King Badis (work beginning in 1057).

Its layout comprises two walled areas, one inside the other. The inner walled area contains a palace which now houses a small and interesting archaeological museum – ceramics in particular.

The **Alcazaba** was used until 1843 for military and other official uses

(eg Felipe V stayed in the palace when visiting the city).

After 1843 a poor district of the city emerged within and around its walls. Old photos clearly show many poor houses built beside and within the area of the present walls.

From 1931 this whole area underwent the very substantial restoration (perhaps 'rebuilding' is a better term) which can presently be seen, under architect Antonio Palacios Ramilo and historian **Juan Temboury Alvarez** (1899–1965) (whose bust can be seen beside the entrance to the monument).

On leaving the Alcazaba turn sharp left up a one–way street – Paseo de Juan Temboury.

This soon bends to the left, where you take a fork to the left, and walk uphill along the foot of the Alacazaba walls.

At the end of the Alcazaba wall you will see a flight of steps.

Take these steps. They lead to a sloping path, which zigs left and then zags right. Cross to six steps and a further sloping path.

This will take you to the **Castillo del Gibralfaro** – up an admittedly rather steep path, but with the reward of quite spectacular views of the city, the port and the sea.

Half way up this path there is a viewing platform.

After resting at the viewing platform, continue uphill.

Near the top the path forks. You can take either route. They both end at the car park to the Castillo del Gibralfaro.

Turn left within the car park and visit the Castillo de Gibralfaro.

On leaving the Gibralfaro turn to the left and walk down the tree–lined road.

Castillo del Gibralfaro

The word 'Gibralfaro' seems to come from a combination of the Arabic 'yabel' (mountain) and the Greek ' faruh' (lighthouse), suggesting an original maritime navigation function.

The present fortification, no doubt replacing earlier structures, dates from 1333-4, and was built by the Moorish leader Yusuf I of Granada.

Following the introduction into military combat of artillery shelling at around this time it would have provided more appropriate fortification than the lower–positioned Alcazaba

There is a linking walled passage–way ('coracha') between the Alcazaba and the Gibralfaro, although this is not open to the public.

Within the Gibralfaro is an interesting museum with many old prints and plans showing the historical development of the city.

This winds down for a few hundred yards or so to a drive to the right which leads to the **Parador** hotel (built in 1928).

Take this drive and admire the views from the Parador.

Go back along the Parador drive to the road, and turn right, so as to begin to walk downhill.

Soon you will see a turn to the left – marked **"Al Tunel"** and **"Puerto Oscura"**.

Take this and follow – for about 15 minutes – this quiet and shady road down through the pine and eucalyptus trees to the rear of the Gibralfaro and Alacazaba.

At the lower end of this road there are in early summer quite spectacular swathes of wild acanthus flowers.

At the very bottom of this road you will see a tunnel.

Go through this – enjoying in summer the ever–present breeze – and at the end take the flight of steps immediately ahead, leading down through the **Gardens of the Puerto Oscura** ('dark gate').

Several routes are possible down these steeply terraced gardens.

Take any route so long as it leads you down to the formal gardens to the left of the Town Hall – the **Jardines de Pedro Luis Alonso**.

At the bottom of the Gardens of the Puerto Oscura, cross the road to the Town Hall Gardens.

The Town Hall Gardens – Jardines de Pedro Luis Alonso

These formal Mediterranean gardens were designed by Strachan and laid out in 1945. They were named after the first mayor of Malaga following the Civil War.

Walk left through these gardens, and across the road at the far end you will see a glass and metal structured building – the **Municipal Art Gallery**.

Municipal Art Gallery – Museo del Patrimonio Municipal

Closed Mondays.
Open, Summer, Tues–Sun 11–21 hrs; Winter, Tues–Sun 10–20 hrs.

This Gallery contains a selection of the city's large collection of paintings (the remainder of which are in due course to be hung in the Aduana–Customs House building). The main collection is to be found on the upper floors, where there are also rooms with interesting prints of old Malaga.

As you exit the Town Hall Gardens take a series of six linked pedestrian crossings, across a busy traffic intersection.

At the end of the sixth pedestrian crossing, walk along under a deeply–shaded avenue of trees.

This is **Paseo de Reding** – a street containing very fine 19th century mansions.

On your right – just before the Bullring – is the **Hospital Noble**.

Hospital Noble

This building dates from 1867 and takes its name from **Dr Joseph Noble**, an Englishman who died in Malaga of cholera in 1861 – his heirs subsequently donating money for the establishment of a hospital for local people and for sailors of all nationalities. The building currently houses municipal offices.

The story of Dr Noble is told in Part Two of this Guide.

 Pass by Hospital Noble and approach the **Bullring**.

Walk beside it, keeping it to your right.

The **Bullring Museum** is depicted as being at Puerto No 8, but in fact it is entered through Puerto No 9. Enter there and go up the staircase to the first floor.

Exit the Bullring Museum and turn right, continuing along Paseo Reding's shady avenue of finely pleached trees.

Look out for number 20 on the right: the **Palacio de la Tinta** – dating from 1920 (designed by Julio O'Brien,

for the Andalucian Railway Company).

Look across the road also at Numbers 41– 43, from which an idea can be gained of the original grandeur of this street.

Malaga Bullring and Museum

Open 10.00–13.00 and 17.00– 22.00

The Bullring dates from 1874–6 and was designed in neo–mudejar style by Joaquin Rucoba.

It is dedicated to **Antonio Ordoñez**, one of Spain's most famous bullfighters. Born in Ronda in 1932, he made his first public appearance as a bullfighter in 1948, and in 1951 (aged 19) he fought in the bullring in Madrid. In the glittering career which followed, Ordoñez came face to face with over 1000 bulls. He finally retired in 1968, having fought over 60 bullfights in that year alone. Ordonez' father was also a bull–fighter and through that connection the young Ordonez knew Ernest Hemingway. In later years Ordonez was a friend of the American actor Orson Welles, and when Welles died in 1987, his ashes were scattered on Antonio's estate near Ronda. Ordonez himself died in 1998.

Continue along, and after about 200–300 metres look out for a gateway on the left with two – quite small – lion statues on the stone gate–posts.

This is the **English Cemetery**, which if open should be explored.

The English Cemetery

Closed Mondays. Open Tues–Sat 9.30–2.30; Sun 11.00–14.00.

This cemetery was established in 1831, and its story is told later in this Guide.

For the moment the words of **Hans Christian Andersen**, who visited in 1862, are worth setting out:

"...I wandered in a little paradise, this charming garden. Here were myrtle hedges, covered with flowers sufficient for a thousand bridal wreaths; high geranium bushes growing round the tombstones, which had inscriptions in Danish – Norse, it might also be called, as these were inscriptions over men from the north; there were English, German and Dutch to be read. Passion flowers flung their tendrils over many gravestones, pepper–trees waved their drooping branches amidst this place of repose. Here stood a single palm, there a gum tree, and in the centre of all this vegetation was a neat, small house, within which refreshments were to be had; pretty children with laughing eyes were playing there. The whole cemetery was encircled by a hedge of wild cacti, over which one beheld the wide, heaving ocean."

Not much has changed.

For more information about the English Cemetery see Part Two of this Guide.

On leaving the English Cemetery, cross over Paseo de Reding.

Turn right, and then immediately left, and follow this road towards the sea.

On your right is a building which incorporated until recently the **Courts of Justice**.

Courts of Justice

Built between 1921 to 1926, to designs by the architect Strachan, this was originally the **Hotel Principe de Asturia** and later the **Hotel Miramar**. It was for a time also a hospital before more recently being home of the **Courts of Justice**. It is currently undergoing redevelopment and is expected to become again a hotel.

Cross – very carefully – over the busy coastal dual carriage-way and you arrive at the coastal promenade: the Paseo Maritima.

You now have a choice of routes:

- a good long walk to the left along the coast (the promenade runs for many miles), or
- a short walk (about five minutes) to the right to return to our starting–point, **La Farola**.

If you feel energetic and take the former option, just turn left and keep walking!

As you walk along the city beach you will pass a preserved tramcar, built in 1905 for use in San Francisco and subsequently used until the 1960s in the streets of Malaga. If your energy levels are still high, try out the free gym equipment on the sea-ward side of the tramcar – if energy levels are low, just sit and admire the view back to the port. After your workout or rest continue along the promenade.

After a few more minutes (at **Balneario del Carmen**, an establishment of somewhat faded glory, but soon to be rejuvenated with the development of a substantial sea–water pool) the path leaves the sea–front for about 200 metres, after which it is again possible to return to the seafront. This is the 'village' of **Pedregalejo**.

Immediately you are able to return to the sea–front, look to your right and you will see a boat repair yard called **Astilleros Nereo**.

There is, inside, a wonderful museum devoted to the history of boat–building, and containing a large number of model replicas of historic ships. The entrance door is not always open – but ring the bell or knock on the door, and you will receive a friendly welcome.

From here continue along past numerous local bars, cafes and restaurants.

In about an hour you will reach, at **El Palo**, a coastal promontory and a yacht club. Just before you get to the yacht club is the famous **El Tintero II** fish restaurant. This comes alive at weekends when many hundreds of Malaguenans visit for lunch. No menus. Just find a table, order a drink, and then catch the eye of waiters as they carry round plates of different seafood. The final bill is just a matter of assessing the debris on your table. Different sizes and types of plates cost different amounts: so be warned before beckoning over the waiter with the silver platter!

To return to Malaga you have two choices: walk back the way you came, or head inland a couple of hundred yards and take an air–conditioned bus (number 11).

Contents

THE STORY OF GENERAL TORRIJOS*

In the summer of 1830, a raggle–taggle company of conspirators, dedicated to the overthrow of the tyrannical King Ferdinand VII of Spain, began to assemble in Gibraltar. They came singly and in pairs, like scattered raindrops struggling to become a storm; a threadbare band of idealists for whom Fate was already preparing cataclysmic failure and death.

Their story is well–known, due in part to the celebrity of some of its peripheral characters, like Alfred Tennyson and Thomas Carlyle. Yet at its heart lies a mystery that is hardly considered. Somewhere along the line it seems clear that the conspirators were betrayed. The question is, by whom?

Ferdinand VII, son of Charles IV, came to the Spanish throne in March 1808 when the beleaguered Charles abdicated in his favour. Within weeks Napoleon Bonaparte, intent on consolidating his occupation of the country, engineered the removal of both and gave the throne to his brother, Joseph. Ferdinand was bunged into a French prison and stayed there until the Spanish ousted their occupiers in 1814. Ferdinand returned home in triumph and repaid his people by installing himself as a brutal, autocratic

*This section follows very closely, and with the author's permission – for which, our thanks – the wonderfully vivid account given by Dave Wood on the website: thegibraltarmagazine.com.

Antonio Gisbert Perez (1835 – 1901): Oil painting, 1888: Prado, Madrid.

dictator. In the words of one historian, Ferdinand was 'the most contemptible king in Spanish history'. Sometimes, it seems, you just can't win.

The problem with a king throwing his weight around like a pompadoured playground bully is that people tend to resent it. And deprived of the opportunity to deliver a weighty kick to his pantalooned posterior on election day, they look for other ways to unseat him. Violent ways.

The hour produces the man, and the man selected by destiny for an early morning wake–up call was **General José Maria de Torrijos y Uriarte**, scion of a noble family, and a distinguished soldier. Torrijos took part in an unsuccessful coup attempt in 1817, and was imprisoned for his pains. On his release in 1823 he tried again, and after lighting a second damp squib, fled with his wife to England. In London he made gloriously impractical plans to raise a revolutionary army and return to deliver the final crushing blow to Ferdinand.

The impractical plans of idealists are irresistible to youth and to poets. Torrijos was soon a familiar man about town, and his cause attracted many influential friends, including a shadowy group of Cambridge University intellectuals known as The Apostles. Among them was a young man named John Sterling whose father, Captain Edward Sterling, owned a house in London to which Torrijos was regularly invited. It was there that he met the essayist and historian, Thomas Carlyle, the poet Alfred Tennyson and others of the social and intellectual elite.

Torrijos' ideas were romantic and inspiring, but he lacked the funds to turn them into action. John Sterling had the answer. He had an Irish cousin, **Robert Boyd** from Ballymacool, in now Northern Ireland, who on the face of it appears to have been barmy. He had resigned his commission in the Indian Army on receiving an inheritance of four thousand pounds and, with the money burning a hole in his pocket, returned to England intent on buying a ship and starting a new career as a pirate in the Philippines. Sterling took him aside and suggested that instead he throw in his lot with Torrijos. Torrijos, for his part, assured Boyd that on the overthrow of Ferdinand, he would be rewarded with the colonelcy of a Spanish cavalry regiment. It was all half an inch from lunacy, but they were young and not to know. In 1962 they would have strummed guitars and sung 'The Times They Are A–Changin'. In

1830 the best they could do was to make plans to slay a tyrant.

With Boyd's money they bought a ship, moored it in the Thames and stocked it with arms. At last their pipe dreams were emerging from the smoke. Soon they would sail to Spain with fifty hand– picked men.

Once there that fifty would become hundreds, then thousands as the people rose in support. Ferdinand's days were numbered.

Suddenly, as they were riding the crest of a euphoric wave, a veritable adrenalin tsunami, John Sterling did a curious thing. He got cold feet. Writing in 1937, author Graham Greene attributes this to the sudden intrusion of cold reality into hot dreams. According to Greene, "his health gave way and furnished him with an excuse to stay behind". Others say the excuse was a sudden decision to get married. The only certainty is that he abruptly withdrew from the scheme and played no further part. Curiously, only days later, the British authorities, goaded by the Spanish envoy, seized the ship and prevented it from sailing.

Scattered to the wind like so much thistledown the conspirators drifted to Gibraltar to regroup and rethink. Tennyson was still committed to the cause, but he and another Englishman, Arthur Hallam, travelled instead to the Pyrenees to deliver funds to like–minded rebels in the north.

In Gibraltar, time weighed heavy upon the increasingly aimless group. Three times they made abortive attempts to kick–start the revolution, attacking San Roque, Estepona and La Línea, which they "captured" and held for a few hours, but when the inhabitants resolutely refused to rally to their flag they dispiritedly withdrew.

Nevertheless, their continued presence in Gibraltar placed an increasing strain on Anglo–Spanish relations. The British envoy in Madrid, Henry Addington, and the Prime Minister, Lord Palmerston, wanted desperately to see the back of them. Given time it might have happened through natural wastage. Most of the British recruits tired of hanging around twiddling their thumbs and melted away. Eventually only the hard core, including Robert Boyd, remained. Eager to be free of them, the government offered passage to voluntary exile anywhere in the world, save Gibraltar and Spain. They refused.

Suddenly, Torrijos received a letter from Málaga, purportedly from his second–in–command, "Viriato", but now considered a forgery. It claimed that 2500 troops were poised to take up arms against Ferdinand and anxiously awaiting Torrijos' arrival to lead them. Torrijos wanted to believe it, so he did. On 30th November 1831 he and his band set sail for Málaga. They should have become suspicious when a previously friendly coastguard captain fired on them near Fuengirola, but with judgment vanquished by hope they pressed on.

Then driven onto the rocks by a Spanish Customs Cutter they put to shore, abandoned ship and moved into the hills to begin their march on Málaga. On December 5th they reached Alhaurín de la Torre, and suddenly found themselves surrounded by troops led by the governor, González Moreno. They came not – as Torrijos had hoped and expected – to join the conspirators, but to arrest them.

They were roped together and

marched to Málaga's Carmelite monastery and held there pending instructions from the Secretary of Defence in Madrid. The presence of Robert Boyd was reported to the British Consul, William Mark, but he was not allowed to see him. The word from Madrid, when it came, was uncompromising. All 52 prisoners, including the innocent 15–year old cabin boy, were to be shot immediately. They were taken from the monastery on the day after their arrest to the Playa de San Andrés and executed on the beach. Wiiliam Mark took charge of Boyd's body; and on the following morning Boyd became the first person to be interred in Málaga's new English Cemetery.

Addington, his eyes brimming with crocodile tears, wrote a feeble letter of "protest" to the Spanish, acknowledging that Boyd deserved his fate, but weakly suggesting that he might have been given a trial first.

On any reading of the events of 1830 and 1831, it is clear that the conspirators' every movement was known both in London and Madrid. Somewhere in their midst, surely, was a spy.

Carlyle wrote freely about the affair, but it is odd that Tennyson, who showed with The Charge of The Light Brigade that he had a penchant for the futile military fiasco, never referred to it at all. Odder still was the reaction of John Sterling. Torrijos and his comrades may have been naïvely idealistic and doomed from the start, but they were fighting for a just cause, and they had died for it. No–one connected with the plan need have felt any shame. Many would have trumpeted it with pride, and vowed to carry on the fight. Yet Sterling forever afterwards forbade the name of Torrijos to be mentioned in his presence. Why Torrijos? Why not the names of Addington? Palmerston? King Ferdinand?

Greene may have been right. Sterling's abrupt withdrawal from the venture may have been due to ill health. It may equally have been due to his impending marriage or to simple cowardice. He would not be the first or the last strident revolutionary who, at the moment of truth, turned out to be all mouth and trousers. But if any of these were true his subsequent actions become inexplicable. An hysterical aversion to hearing the name Torrijos suggests feelings of guilt far deeper than any rooted in the knowledge that, but for illness, he might have died on the Playa de San Andrés too. And a coward would have turned the thing to advantage by loudly proclaiming so as the port made its after–dinner rounds. But a man whose betrayal of his friends had led directly to the deaths of 51 men and a boy, including his own cousin, might well have difficulty coming to terms with the knowledge. Such a man might easily try to erase the past for the sake of his own sanity.

And what of the shadowy "Viriato", from whom we never hear again, and whose real identity was said to be known only to Torrijos and another high–ranking conspirator named Flores Calderón? In 1831 letters were not typed, let alone sent via text–messaging. If Torrijos received a letter allegedly from Viriato, it is relatively safe to assume that he would have been familiar with his "second–in–command's" hand writing.

The bland assumption that the letter was a forgery begs many questions. In order to imitate Viriato's hand writing, the forgers (Spanish? British? Both?) would have needed a sample of the real thing. And to make the letter's tales of friendly troops waiting to rebel credible, they had to know that Viriato himself would not be in a position to contradict it. They had to know exactly where he was, and that he would stay there. In prison, or spending thirty pieces of silver in the bordellos of Málaga?

Ferdinand survived a number of further coup attempts and died in Madrid on 29th September 1833. But the rebels had the last, posthumous laugh. Tyrants can kill men, but they cannot kill ideas. Just down the road from the cemetery

where his friend Robert Boyd lies, people mingle today in the sunshine in the Plaza del General Torrijos.

The matter remained one of some public controversy. In the summer of 1834 Governor Moreno made a visit to England during which there were demands in Parliament that he be arrested and tried for the 'murder' of Robert Boyd. Palmerston answered that no British court had jurisdiction and, in any event the circumstances of the raid 'took the case of Mr Boyd out of the protection of the law of nations'.

THE ENGLISH CEMETERY*

Before the opening of this cemetery the death of a protestant in Spain presented, in the words of Marjorie Grice–Hutchinson, a 'gruesome problem'. Protestants, being deemed heretics, had been denied burial in Catholic churchyards and cemeteries. In 1622, she relates, the English Ambassador's secretary died at Santander and was not allowed to be buried. Instead the coffined corpse was thrown into the sea, 'but no sooner was the ambassador gone than the fishermen, fearing for their catch for so long as the coffin of a heretic lay in their waters, dragged it up again and threw it back on to the land.'

Following similar difficulty following the death (by assassinaton) in 1650 of Cromwell's envoy. Ascham, Cromwell moved that a treaty be agreed between the two countries which would, amongst other things deal with this issue. In 1667 such a treaty was agreed and provided, in Article 35, that a 'decent and convenient burial place shall be granted and appointed to bury the bodies of [British] subjects … who die … in Spain'. This principle was subsequently ratified and confirmed by the treaties of Utrecht (1713), Madrid (1715 and 1721) and Versailles (1783).

Unfortunately, the provisions within these treaties were not for a long while implemented. And so, in Malaga, the burial of a protestant remained a harrowing process.

Grice–Hutchinson explains:

"Their bodies were not permitted to be interred by day, but had to be taken down to the sea–shore at night by light of a torch, and there buried in an upright position in the sand. Besides being exposed to being torn up by dogs or washed out to sea by the waves, the corpses were still further insulted by the dumping of every sort of refuse and ordure in the vicinity of their resting–place".

*The following account draws very closely from an article published by the late Dr Frank Griffith Dawson, and from a privately published book by the late Marjorie Grice–Hutchison (Baroness von Schlippenbach), historian of economic thought of southern Europe and local benefactor. Grice–Hutchinson spent more than half her life in and around Malaga. She was a frequent visitor to her father's local farm in the 1930s and witnessed the outbreak in 1936 of the Civil War. She and her father helped numerous Spaniards to flee to Gibraltar on their yacht, returning with much needed medicines and food. She settled in Malaga in the mid–1950s. On her death she donated her farm – San Julian – to the University of Malaga, where it now comprises the Centro de Experimentacion Grice–Hutchinson. She received honours in Spain for her social work (the Orden de Merito Civil) and also received from Queen Elizabeth II an OBE.

THE ENGLISH CEMETERY

Things changed as a consequence of the activities of the British Consul in Malaga, Robert Mark.

Born in 1782 at Berwick–on–Tweed, Mark began work in the textile industry. However, when the business he was in failed to thrive he, aged 18, joined the navy – where his understanding of basic accountancy helped him win a series of promotions – such that at the age of only 19 he was invited by Nelson to join the latter at dinner. Indeed, Mark served under Nelson on the Victory for a few months.

With the Peninsular War at its height, Mark became an agent in Gibraltar to naval captains responsible for the condemnation and sale of prizes they had captured; a position of authority which he held until the war ended in 1815.

In 1816 Mark moved with his wife and family to Malaga with a view to becoming British Consul, a post he took when it became vacant in 1824 – the elderly incumbent having lived rather longer than anticipated. However, these eight years in wait were significant. In his journal Mark tells of his disgust when driving along the coast with his family and having to pass the spot where bodies were buried 'feet–foremost'.

On becoming Consul, Mark was himself called upon to perform a burial service for a Protestant clerk at the consular office. His plea to the Governor of Malaga to be allowed to bury the body on land went unanswered as the hour of the funeral arrived. Much disappointed, Mark sought to secure at least some dignity for the event.

Grice–Hutchison describes the scene:

"Arrayed in full uniform, Mark proceeded to the house of the dead man, and there formed a procession made up of himself and his vice–consul, along with the coffin (covered by a Union Jack and carried by six captains of British vessels), the American consul, all the respectable body of British residents, captains and sailors, the Consul's servant with the Prayer Book, and a train of friends. The Consul's carriage brought up the rear. The cortège thus formed began its march towards the place of interment, followed by a curious crowd.

On the way they passed some Canons of the cathedral, who stood looking on in surprise. Mark took off his hat and saluted them very conspicuously, a ceremony which was instantly followed by the whole procession. [The Canons] could do no less than return by doffing their big hats, [their heads] remaining uncovered until the cortege had passed. Mark continued on his way complacent at having contrived to get at least this semi–official mark of respect paid to the body of his dead countryman.

On reaching the hillside where he hoped to find the grave prepared, Mark was disappointed to see that it had been dug on the beach. There being no time for consideration, the mourners wended their way to the sands. Mark took up his station at the head of the grave and read the Service for the Dead as well as his agitation would allow. But he faltered – he trembled and shook, and covered the Book with tears, the flowing of which he could not prevent…. When it was all over, Mark drove home very much exhausted and overcome, but feeling an inexpressible satisfaction at having achieved all this in broad daylight instead of at the dead hour of night."

As time went by Mark became quite obsessed by the need for a proper burial place. In due course, in 1829, he petitioned General Jose Manso, Governor of Malaga, and was gratified by the Governor's sympathetic response. Manso convened a meeting of the Board of Health, which Mark addressed; following which the Governor cut

short discussion and ordered that a 'place be made over to you for the purpose of decently burying your dead'.

It was then said, somewhat mischievously, that Mark began to look around to see who might become the first occupant of this cemetery. The contemporary travel writer Richard Ford (whose work is quoted later in this Guide) liked to joke that Mark was eyeing Ford's 'pretty but ailing' wife as a first customer. In fact the first to be buried was a George Stephens, the owner of a brig, the Cicero, who accidentally drowned in Malaga harbour.

In 1831 the wall to the cemetery was constructed. It appears that to be able to dig the foundations of the wall, the wall was built slightly inside the boundary of the plot, with Stephens' grave remaining outside the wall.

When the cemetery was opened a plaque was placed over the entrance 'recording the royal permission, and above that a cross'. According to Ford the Malaguenos were "amazed when they beheld this emblem of Christianity raised over the last home of Lutheran dogs".

Today the amazement has long abated and the heavy wrought iron entrance gates are now flanked by two pillars atop each of which sits a lion with a forepaw resting on a stone globe.

The first to be buried within the walls was Robert Boyd of Londonderry, an idealistic young army officer who foolishly enlisted in an expedition led by an exiled Spanish general to overthrow despotic King Ferdinand. With his Spanish companions he was quickly apprehended shortly after landing at Malaga and summarily shot on the 11th December 1831, "in the sacred cause of liberty", according to his monument's inscription, "aged twenty six". This summary execution of a British subject provoked a political storm in London. Questions were asked in Parliament, and the press railed against the reactionary Spanish monarch.

Richard Ford was in Spain at the time of Boyd's execution and, on January 11th 1832, wrote to his friend Henry Addington, British Envoy Extraordinary and Plenipotentiary in Madrid, that Mark:

> *"is gone wild about the Malaga events and the execution of Mr. Boyd."*

Four months later, the painter and future Royal Academician, David Roberts (see further, below), spent three weeks with the Mark family during an extensive sketching trip in Spain. According to Mark's journal, he took Roberts on a tour of the cemetery where – observing the pains Mark was taking to improve the situation, by planting trees in the adjoining ground, and thereby forming an agreeable promenade – Roberts made a drawing which he transferred to a lithographic stone so that Mark might have numerous copies made.

Mark extended his hospitality to many other visitors, both living and dead, until his death in 1849, when he joined Boyd and his companions in the 'sepulchral museum'.

Mark's monument, one of the cemetery's most prominent memorials, is a tall, fluted column surmounted by an urn draped with a mourning cloth. Erected by his widow, the inscription (on the large, rectangular block upon which the column is based) modestly records that Mark was born in Berwick on Tweed on 6th March 1782 and died at Alhaurin, a village near Malaga on 13th January 1849. It does not recount his rise from humble beginnings, his distinguished career in the Royal Navy or his service under Nelson. Nor does the inscription inform us, as his great grandson subsequently revealed, that he was known as 'Old Pomposo' in Malaga where his

insistence on regularity in the life of his household became a byword – and where it was humorously observed that his wife produced his offspring always at regular intervals.

Meanwhile the cemetery's fame as a 'must' for the tourist itinerary was assured when in 1845 John Murray in London published Richard Ford's two volume 'Handbook for Travellers in Spain' to wide critical acclaim. Despite its price, small print and its length (over 1600 pages), 389 copies were sold in the first three months and it quickly became an essential accompaniment for English travellers daring to venture south of the Pyrenees into Spain, that land of brigands and civil war.

Ford's sense of humour is evident throughout. He urged travellers to Malaga to visit the cemetery:

"because it was the first permitted in our times for the repose of our heretical carcasses, which used to be buried in the sea sands like dead dogs, and below the low water mark; and even this concession offended orthodox fishermen, who feared that their soles might become infected."

William Mark's son, and successor as Consul, continued the care and embellishment of the cemetery with the planting of palms, eucalyptus, yucca, plumbago, wisteria and jasmine so that by the 1850's it had become a popular gathering place for the living as well as the dead.

The mining engineer and geologist, Captain S. E. Widrington of the Royal Navy, wrote of the cemetery that:

"It is impossible to conceive any thing prettier than this spot, which is resorted to in the fine evenings, not only by resident foreigners, but by great numbers of Malagueños who have sufficient taste and liberality to admire both the arrangement and the object of it."

In 1862 Hans Christian Andersen was so entranced after visiting the cemetery that he recalled he had:

"walked in a most lovely garden.

Here were myrtle hedges with blooms for thousands of bridal wreaths; tall geranium bushes encircled memorial tablets. Passion flowers twined their tendrils over many gravestones and pepper trees drooped their weeping branches over many a resting place. Here stood a solitary palm, there a rubber tree. Pretty children with laughing eyes played there. The whole garden is encircled by a hedge of wild cactus, over which one looks down to the broad, rolling sea."

The cemetery was gradually expanded and by December 1900 could accommodate the mass burial of the officers and men of the Imperial German Navy's training ship 'Gneisenau' who died when that ship sank just outside Málaga harbour.

Some forty years later four other bodies recovered from the sea were brought to this hillside to be re–interred following earlier burial at Marbella – an Australian Royal Air Force Flying Officer, a Royal Navy Commander and two RAF radio operators – air gunner Sergeants. Their white headstones lie in a single neat row, side by side, in a white–gravelled rectangle a few yards away from Robert Boyd's memorial.

Today, a busy avenida and a solid bulwark of square apartment blocks cuts off the cemetery from beach and sea. The view is therefore no longer 'glorious' as it was when described in 1865 by O'Shea in his Guide to Spain. Moreover, the hillside above sprouts yet more concrete apartment rectangles. Nevertheless, the cemetery with its well–tended trees, shrubs and flowering plants still remains an island of tranquillity amidst the surrounding urban sprawl, and offers visitors encouraging reminders of past endurance, faith and sacrifice.

Hans Christian Andersen would still very much enjoy his 'favourite place'.

THE WRECK OF THE GNEISENAU

The Gneisenau was a three–masted steam turbine frigate used for training naval cadets and cabin boys.

It had a crew of 466: made up of 19 officers, 51 naval cadets, 186 sailors and 210 cabin boys

It arrived in the port of Malaga between November 13th and 15th 1900. Its presence in the area was part of a general mission connected with the protection of German interests in Morocco, at that time undergoing some political turbulence.

Whilst present the ship engaged in some canon–firing practice – doing so at anchorage outside the harbour.

Over the next few weeks there was much free time for shore–leave for the crew, including sightseeing visits to Granada. The crew became familiar figures in the town, mixing with the local German community, and there was even a civic reception organised on board ship.

On the morning of Sunday December 16th, when anchored outside the harbour, a storm brew up – and by ten in the morning the winds had reached 100 kms per hour.

Despite local recommendation to return to within the harbour's protection, the commander of the vessel opted at 10.40 am to weigh anchor and manoeuvre under engine power away from the harbour, and so confront the storm a safe distance away from land.

But at 10.50 am the steam engines lost power, and the ship was blown by the easterly wind towards the rocks forming the harbour breakwater some 800 metres away. With the wind still gaining force an attempt was made to drop anchor, but to no avail – the anchors gaining no purchase from the rocky seabed.

At 11.05 am the vessel hit the breakwater rocks and the engine–room immediately flooded. The ship sank twenty minutes later, at 11.25 a.m.

Soon the bells of the Cathedral and the churches of San Juan, the Martyrs, Carmen and Santiago rang out the alarm that some disaster was occurring. People ran down the streets towards the harbour and witnessed the tragedy unfolding. Valiant attempts were

made to get close to the stricken vessel but this was difficult owing to the strength of the storm.

Forty–one crew members together with their Commander were killed in the shipwreck; and twelve Malaguenos who had gone to rescue also lost their lives.

Although a number of the crew were not at the time aboard (it being Sunday those who were Catholics had gone ashore to mass) there were said to have been more than 200 crew members tossed around in the turbulent waters.

Many of the survivors were taken into the homes of local people to recuperate from their ordeal; and in a number of cases friendships developed which blossomed into marriage. The classical composer Emilio Lehmberg Ruiz was the son of the marriage between a crew survivor (Emilio Otto Lehmberg Tielecke) and the daughter (Concepción Ruiz Rodríguez) of a family which offered Emilio shelter.

The actions of the Malaguenos resulted in due course in Queen Maria Cristina, in name of her son Alfonso XIII, subsequently granting to the city of Malaga the title of "Very Hospitable", and this forms to this day a part of the City's official shield.

THE FLOODS OF 1907 AND THE STORY OF THE GERMAN BRIDGE

To the story of the wreck of the Gneisenau there is a sequel.

Just a few years later, on the night between the 23rd and 24th September 1907, there was torrential rain. Again, the church bells rang to sound the alarm. Flood water running down the Rio Guadalmedina resulted in extensive flooding of the Trinidad and Perchel districts. A bridge upstream of the present German Bridge collapsed and was carried down to crash into the Santa Domingo bridge. This too collapsed and the fabric of both bridges was carried further down the river. The next bridge survived, but the blockage caused at that bridge caused the river to divert down the neighbouring avenues towards eventually the port and the sea. A total of 21 people were injured and much property damage was done.

The local German community immediately got together a subscription list and, with contributions from the German State, money was raised to cover the cost of replacing the Santo Domingo bridge, work on which was completed in 1910.

DR JOSEPH NOBLE AND THE FOUNDING OF THE HOSPITAL NOBLE*

Joseph Noble was born in 1798 at Frisby in Leicestershire, and resided at the family home, Danet's Hall, in what is now the Westcotes part of the city centre of Leicester.

Following education at Trinity Hall, Cambridge, Noble returned to Leicester where he became an influential figure. In the December 1835 council elections he was elected a member for

*This account has benefited from information provided by Mr George Spearing in New Zealand.

DR JOSEPH NOBLE AND THE HOSPITAL NOBLE

West St Mary's Ward. In 1839 he was appointed a J.P. and two years later an Alderman. He was elected Mayor in 1858 but resigned the following April to contest the Borough for Parliament for the 'advanced Liberals' – being elected with 1,496 votes. To celebrate this victory some 7,000 people attended a grand open air fête held in the garden of Danet's Hall. Noble evidently did nothing 'by half'.

And he was evidently a force for good. In 1834, he was appointed chairman of the committee to consider the establishment of a new school in the town to take the place of the old Elizabethan grammar school. In 1858, whilst Mayor, Noble was approached by a local solicitor, on behalf of Robert Mackley, a blind man residing in the town, to 'do something' to alleviate the sufferings of the blind. Noble arranged a meeting, attended by himself and 'five other interested gentlemen of the Town'. This led to the formation in 1859 of the 'The Leicester Association for Promoting the General Welfare of the Blind', which, initially under the management of Robert Mackley himself, developed and expanded so that by the end of the Victorian era it had a workshop for blind people and a retail shop. This developed later into the 'The Leicester, Leicestershire and Rutland (Incorporated) Institution for the Blind, to which the word 'Royal' became attached in 1932. Subsequently, in 2001, the Institution was re-branded 'Vista': see www.vista.org.uk.

Noble also donated a number of archaeological discoveries within his estate to the City of Leicester. The story goes that as far back as 1783 part of a Roman mosaic floor was found by chance by Noble's father whilst digging within the cherry orchard on the estate. The find was rather approximately recorded and the discovery not further explored until, in 1850, the Leicester Literary and Philosophical Society took an interest. After much consideration as to the best spot at which to excavate beneath the large ten to twelve acre orchard, there was discovered by iron probe a fine Roman pavement – of altogether different pattern from that preserved in the earlier drawing. This discovery stimulated the interest of the explorers, but further search had to await the spring of 1851. Starting from the newly found pavement, trenches were dug in several directions; and gradually the site of an entire Roman villa was, room by room, laid bare.

The floors were mostly covered with mosaics. But again, none showed the recorded pattern of the particular pavement for which the search had been instituted. It was only later, when the plan of the villa had almost entirely been revealed, that the mosaic first unearthed in 1783 was found: it being the floor of a terrace running along the whole of the front of the villa, at least 120 feet in length and 11 feet in width.

Great care was taken to avoid accident or damage to this discovery – policemen guarded the spot by day and night until it was possible to transfer the finest portion of the pavement, at Dr Noble's request, to what is now the Leicester Jewry Wall Museum. A semi–circular part of the mosaic was triumphantly carted in a single piece through the streets of the town, to form one of the most beautiful and interesting objects within that Museum.

Some mosaics from other floors of the villa, were also deposited in the Museum and a plan of the whole

was carefully made. However the remainder of the excavations were reburied: the near city centre site being too valuable in terms of development to remain undeveloped. With time, further redevelopment of this area became necessary, leading to further Roman villa discoveries during the 1970s.

Dr Noble was also known to have been generous in his hospitality at Danet's Hall to persons taking refuge in England from foreign persecution.

But it was Dr Noble's generous spirit which was subsequently to prove his downfall.

In the winter of 1860, while traveling through Spain, and en route between Seville and Pau in the French Pyrenees (where his family had remained) he happened to be in Malaga when an outbreak of cholera occurred. Dr Nobel immediately offered his medical services, but fell victim to the infection and died, aged 63, on 6 January 1861 He was buried in the English Cemetery in Malaga.

At this point the story becomes less clear. It is known that Dr Noble's family provided funds for the building of a hospital in Malaga for the benefit of local people and for sailors of all nationalities. This became – after some delay while the town council reassured themselves that this generous gesture was genuine – Hospital Noble.

The source of funds may have been from the sale the year before (1860) of the Danet's Hall estate in Leicester to the Leicester Freehold Land Society. That Society demolished the Hall in 1861 and prepared the way for the residential development to the immediate west of the Leicester city centre.

The sale of the estate may also have funded, and perhaps also prompted, in 1861, the move of Dr Joseph Noble's son, Mark, to Oamaru, South Island, New Zealand, where in that year he began to build a house based closely on the design of Danet's

circa 1880

Hall. The house, called Casanova – Mark Noble was a life–long bachelor – remains to this day, and is now a restaurant.

In 1861 the North Otago Times carried the following report of a race, mentioning Mark Noble:

> *"The race meeting gathered together a large concourse of people, numbers coming from the other side of the Waitaki river and from Dunedin. Mark Noble … put in an appearance for the first time on this occasion. He attracted a considerable amount of atttention on account of a dispute with regard to the conduct of one of Mr Julius' jockeys. Mr Noble was asked by Mr Reginald Julius to ride the celebrated "Kauri Gum" for the Oamaru Plate, which he did, and won the race. The crowd was fairly orderly, with little of the rowdyism that distinguished New Year's Day. One big burly Maori and a little half –drunken fellow known as English Jack, indulged in a game of fisticuffs, and the … Englishman polished off the native in a few rounds. Creature comforts were supplied by the hotelkeepers from the town, who had carts on the ground. The trivialities attendant on such meetings were provided by a … boy, got up in the most approved style … on the stage ; … broad–ribbed stockings, knee–breeches, scarlet waistcoat, and cut–away frieze coat."*

Mark Noble appears to have left New Zealand to return to Europe in 1865, eventually dying soon after in Malta, and buried at Bagni Di Lucca, Tuscany.

CANOVAS DEL CASTILLO – PRIME MINISTER AND PROMOTER OF PASEO DEL PARQUE

Cánovas Del Castillo was one of the most important of Spain's nineteenth century politicians.

He was born in Malaga in 1828 and educated in the city. Then, following the death of his father, he moved to Madrid to live with his uncle, the writer Serafín Estébanez Calderón.

He studied law at the University of Madrid, but showed rather more early interest in politics and Spanish history.

His active involvement in politics dates from the 1854 revolution led by the General Leopoldo O'Donell (of Irish ancestry, and later three times Prime Minister of Spain). This led him to write the 'Manifiesto de Manzanares', a document which accompanied the military overthrow of the sitting government and laid out the political goals of the revolutionary movement.

During the final years of Isabel II, he served in a number of posts, including a diplomatic mission to Rome, governor of Cádiz, and director general of local administration. This period of his political career culminated in his being twice made a government minister, taking the interior portfolio in 1864 and then the overseas territories portfolio in 1865–1866.

After the 1868 Glorious Revolution (Revolución Gloriosa), he retired from the Government, although he was a strong supporter of the restoration of the Bourbon monarchy during the First Spanish Republic (1873–1874) and, as the leader of the conservative minority in the Cortes, he declaimed against universal suffrage and freedom of religion.

He returned to active politics with the 1874 overthrow of the Republic by General Martínez Campos and the elevation of Isabell II's son Alfonso XII to the throne.

He served as Prime Minister for six years, starting in 1874 (although he was twice briefly replaced, in 1875 and 1879). During this period, he was a principal author of the Spanish Constitution of 1876, a document which formalised the constitutional monarchy that had resulted from the restoration of Alfonso XII, and restricted electoral suffrage in order to reduce the political influence of the working class.

Cánovas Del Castillo played a key role in bringing an end to the last Carlist threat to Bourbon authority by merging a group of dissident Carlist deputies with his own Conservative party. And after 1881 an artificial two–party system designed to reconcile the competing militarist, Catholic and Carlist power bases led to an alternating prime ministership with the progressive Práxedes Mateo Sagasta.

He assumed the functions of the Head of State during the regency of María Cristina following Alfonso's death in 1885.

However, by the late 1880s, Cánovas Del Castillo's policies were under threat from two sources.

First, his overseas policy was becoming increasingly untenable. A policy of repression against Cuban

nationalists was ineffective and Spain's authority was challenged seriously by the 1895 rebellion led by José Martí. Spain's policy against Cuban independence brought her increasingly into conflict with the United States, an antagonism that culminated, a year after Canovas del Castillo's death, in the Spanish–American War of 1898 (where Spain lost her final American colonies – eg Puerto Rico – as well as Guam and the Phillipines).

Second, the politically repressed working class was growing increasingly troublesome, and pressure for expanded suffrage mounted amid widespread discontent over electoral manipulation.

Cánovas Del Castillo eventually paid a high personal price for his policies of repression. The immediate background can be traced to June 1896, when a bomb was thrown during the Corpus Christi procession in Barcelona. This attack precipitated an aggressive reprisal by government against Spanish anarchists, socialists and republicans. Some four hundred alleged revolutionaries were jailed at the Montjuïc Fortress, overlooking Barcelona; and many of these died as a result of torture inflicted. Of eighty–seven prisoners taken to court, only eight eventually received death sentences and just nine were condemned to long imprisonment. The other seventy–one were declared innocent, but on the orders of Canovas del Castillo, were deported anyway to Río de Oro, a Spanish colony in West Africa.

A wish for revenge for the Montjuïc persecutions led Michele Angiolillo, an Italian anarchist, to travel to Spain from London under false identity. Angiolillo finally found Cánovas alone at the thermal bath resort of Santa Águeda (now a psychiatric hospital), in Mondragón, Guipúzcoa, on the 8th

August 1897, and shot him dead. The Prime Minister's wife hurried to the scene, shouting "Murderer! Murderer!". Angiolillo, it is said, bowed and declared, "Pardon, Madame. I respect you as a lady, but I regret that you were the wife of that man."

Angiolillo allowed the authorities to capture him. It is likely that he hoped thereby to prevent the Spanish government from using the search for Canovas' killer as an excuse for a heavier repression. He was executed by garotte on the 20th August in the nearby town of Vergara.

Throughout his political life Cánovas Del Castillo was an active 'man of letters'. His historical writings earned him a considerable reputation, particularly his History of the Decline of Spain (Historia de la decadencia de España), for which he was elected at the young age of 32 to the Real Academia de la Historia in 1860. This was followed by elevation to other bodies of letters, including the Real Academia Española in 1867, the Academia de Ciencias Morales y Políticas in 1871 and the Academia de Bellas Artes de San Fernando in 1887. He also served as the head of the Athenaeum in Madrid (1870–74, 1882–84 and 1888–89).

DAVID ROBERTS – LANDSCAPE AND ARCHITECTURAL ARTIST

David Roberts was born in Edinburgh in 1796. The son of a shoemaker he was first apprenticed for seven years to a house–decorator, but showed early interest in a rather different form of painting.

He spent his evenings studying art. In 1820 he formed the acquaintance of the celebrated marine painter Clarkson Stanfield, then painting at the Pantheon, Edinburgh, and at Stanfield's suggestion he sent three pictures in 1822 to the Exhibition of Works by Living Artists, held in Edinburgh.

In that same year he moved to London, and gained employment for several years designing and painting theatrical scenery. He worked first for the Coburg Theatre, and later was employed, along with Stanfield, at Drury Lane. In 1824 he exhibited at the British Institution a view of Dryburgh Abbey, and sent two works to the first exhibition of the Society of British Artists, of which he was elected president in 1831. In the same autumn he visited Normandy, and the works which were the results of this excursion began to lay the foundation of his reputation: one of them, a view of Rouen Cathedral, being sold for eighty guineas.

In 1829 he exhibited the "Departure of the Israelites from Egypt", in which his individual style first becomes apparent; three years afterwards he travelled in Spain and Tangiers, returning in the end of 1833 with a supply of effective sketches, elaborated into attractive and popular paintings. His "Interior of Seville Cathedral" was exhibited in the British Institution in 1834, and sold for £300; and he executed a fine series of Spanish illustrations for the *Landscape Annual* of 1836, while in 1837 a selection of his *Picturesque Sketches in Spain* was reproduced by lithography.

It was no less that J.M.W. Turner, who persuaded Roberts to abandon theatrical scene painting and devote himself completely to becoming a true artist. Accordingly, Roberts set sail in 1838 for Egypt and there executed hundreds of drawings and watercolours. Egypt was very much in vogue at this time, and travellers, collectors and lovers of antiquities were very keen to buy works depicting the great monuments of ancient Egypt or inspired by the East. On his return to London, many of these were made into lithographs by Louis Haghe and published in several volumes.

The period 1838–1849 was devoted to the drawings of Egypt and the Middle East. An extensive series of drawings was lithographed by Louis Haghe in *Sketches in the Holy Land and Syria*, 1842–1849.

Such was his reputation that in 1851 he executed, at the request of Queen Victoria, a picture of the opening of the Great Exhibition.

In both 1851 and 1853 Roberts visited Italy, and his last volume of illustrations, *Italy, Classical, Historical and Picturesque*, was published in 1859.

In 1858 he was presented with the freedom of the city of Edinburgh.

The last years of his life were occupied with a series of views of London from the Thames. He was at work upon a picture of St Paul's Cathedral, in November 1864 when – it is said – he died suddenly of 'apoplexy'.

MALAGA – THE UNHAPPY EXPERIENCES OF WILLIAM LITHGOW (1583 – 1645/50)*

The life of William Lithgow is worth relating here as a true tale of travels and adventures not dissimilar to that of his fictional contemporary 'Don Quixote'. His link with the city of Malaga will emerge towards the end of the story.

Lithgow was a Scot, born in the parish of Lanark, in the year 1583. Little is known of his birth or parentage, or of the early period of his life. Indeed it was only the publication of his travels in 1614 that brought him to public notice.

The motives which induced him to leave his native Scotland, and to perform a 'painful and dangerous pilgrimage through foreign lands' are not clear: although he hints, obliquely and tantalisingly, at 'oppression by enemies' as one of the reasons. Ultimately, however, it seems that Lithgow simply had an irresistible desire to visit strange lands; and this clearly became the ruling passion of his life.

He travelled by foot wherever this was possible. He made it a rule, and strictly adhered to it, never to avail himself of any conveyance during a journey when he could accomplish it on foot, and his only departure from this self–imposed rule lay in crossing seas, rivers, or lakes. It is said that during all his travels he never mounted a horse, or put his foot into a carriage, or any description of vehicle whatever.

As a young man, when he was, in his own words, 'yet a stripling', he made two voyages to the "Orcadian and Zetlandian Isles." Shortly after this, he proceeded on a tour through Germany, Bohemia, Helvetia, and the Low countries. From the latter he went to Paris, where he stayed for ten months.

At this point there is no evidence of where Lithgow obtained the funds necessary to support his travels. We may speculate that at this time he trusted in a great measure to the chance casual assistance which he might receive from any of his countrymen whom he might encounter on his way.

A further expedition began in March, 1609, when he was 26. Starting from Paris, Lithgow proceeded directly to Rome. While in Rome he made a narrow escape from the inquisition; the most sanguinary and ferocious of whose members were at that time Scotsmen. Two of these were from St Andrews, and it was from these two fellow countrymen that Lithgow found some difficulty in escaping. This, however, he effected by the assistance of a domestic of the earl of Tyrone, who was then residing at Rome. This man, by the name of Megget, concealed him for three days and nights on the roof of the earl's palace, and, on the fourth night, conveyed him secretly out of the city, by aiding him to scale the walls, as the gates and streets were all carefully guarded by persons appointed by the inquisition to apprehend him.

From Rome Lithgow proceeded to Naples, and from there to Loretto. On his way to the latter place, he met with a carriage, containing two young gentlemen from Rome with their mistresses, all proceeding joyously on a pilgrimage to the shrine of the Madonna. This lively group invited the lonely pedestrian to join them in their carriage for the journey, but, adhering to the rule he had laid down of never availing himself of any such conveyance, Lithgow obstinately refused. At this the good–natured pilgrims descended from their carriage and the whole party jogged merrily on for Loretto.

At Loretto Lithgow fell in with another of his countrymen, of the name of Arthur, a former domestic servant of the earl of Glencairn, who seems to have been imbued with some portion of his own

*Much of the information which follows on William Lithgow has been drawn from the website 'Famous Scots': http://www.electricscotland.com/history/other/lithgow_william.htm

restless and rambling disposition. Having spent some time in Loretto, they proceeded together to Ancona, and thence by sea to Venice. Here his companion left him to cross the Alps, while Lithgow himself moved on to Greece and Asia.

During his travels in Greece and Asia Lithgow encountered particular dangers and difficulties; he was shipwrecked, attacked by bandits, plundered and maltreated, and, with all this, frequently exposed for days and nights together to the inclemency of the weather; his religion excluding him, in several places, not only from the hospitality of the natives, but even from the shelter of their houses.

Not contented with the adventures in which he was unavoidably involved, there were others which he sought out voluntarily. Like the fictional 'Don Quixote' he released captives, or at least assisted them to effect their escape, and came to the aid of distressed damsels. Altogether, Lithgow appears to have been a singularly benevolent and kind–hearted man; ready at all times to peril his life, for the injured or oppressed, whenever he thought such a risk could be of service to them.

From Greece Lithgow proceeded over–land to Egypt, and finally reached Cairo. Whilst in Jerusalem he had the good fortune to fall in with three Dutchmen who were journeying with a caravan in the same direction. These he joined, and kept by them until they reached the Egyptian capital. Here his three companions appear speedily to have killed themselves by drinking an excess of "strong Cyprus wine without mixture of water." Each as they died left the survivors all his property, and the last bequeathed the whole accumulated amount to Lithgow. Lithgow had, however, some difficulty in rescuing his legacy from the grasp of the Venetian consul; but by sacrificing a part he obtained possession of the remainder, which amounted to nine hundred and forty–two zechins of gold, besides rings and tablets.

From Cairo Lithgow proceeded to Alexandria, where he embarked for Malta. From thence he sailed for Sicily, walked from there to Paris, and finally came returned to England, where he presented to King James, to Queen Anne, and to Prince Charles, "certain rare gifts and notable relicks brought from Jordan and Jerusalem."

After remaining in London for about a year, Lithgow's propensity to roving again became too strong to be resisted, and he set out upon another expedition. He now traversed the Netherlands and Switzerland, and from there proceeded to Calabria.

Here another windfall came his way. Between Saramutza and Castello France, he found the dead bodies of two young barons lying in a field, who had just killed each other in a duel. Seeing that they were richly clad, Lithgow searched their pockets and found two silken purses well filled with Spanish pistoles. These he carried off, together with certain rings which they wore on their fingers.

Lithgow moved on to Africa, through Barbary, Morocco, Algiers, Tunis, and Tripoli. Then, crossing over to Italy, he perambulated Hungary, Germany, and Poland, and finally reached Dantzic, where he embarked for England, and once more arrived in safety in London.

By this time Lithgow was an an object of some curiosity and interest, and, while he remained in England, was frequently admitted to audiences with the King, and was a welcomed guest at the tables of the first nobility and gentlemen in the kingdom, where he repaid their civilities by relating the story of his adventures.

Lithgow's spirit of adventure and singular restlessness of disposition, however, were still unsubdued; and neither all that he had seen, nor all that he had suffered, could induce him to settle at home.

In 1619, he again set out on another roving expedition, and on this occasion he was furnished with letters of recommendation from King James, addressed to "all kings,

princes, and dukes." Armed with these documents – which as we shall see proved illusory in terms of protection – he proceeded to Ireland. From there he sailed for France, travelled through Portugal and Spain, and finally arrived at Malaga: so justifying his inclusion in this Guide!

In Malaga Lithgow was apprehended as a spy, and accused of giving intelligence to some English ships which were then on the Spanish coast, on the matter of the return of the plate fleet, carrying back treasure from the Americas.

All poor Lithgow's pleas of innocence availed him nothing, and he was subjected to the most dreadful tortures. It is said that his limbs were mangled and crushed, and his body torn and lacerated with tightened cords and other engines of torture. In due course his innocence as a spy was established to the satisfaction even of his persecutors; but that was not the end of his misfortunes in Malaga.

Released by his political interrogators he was then handed over to the church authorities – to the Inquisition. And from these inquisitors there were inflicted upon him a fresh series of tortures – more horrible than the first.

Maimed and mutilated, Lithgow was at length liberated by the interference of the English consul and of several English residents in Malaga, from whom all knowledge of the unfortunate traveller's fate had been carefully concealed until it was discovered by them by accident.

Shortly after his release he was carried on board an English ship, for his person was so fearfully mangled that he was not only wholly unable to walk, but was apparently beyond hope of recovery. In this state, on his arrival back in England, in 1621, he was exhibited to the King and the whole of the court, lying on a feather bed. His miserable situation excited universal sympathy, and might under a more spirited monarch have become the ground of a national quarrel with the country in which the cruelty and injustice had been inflicted. If his Majesty, however, failed in avenging the unhappy traveller's injuries, he was not wanting in compassion for his sufferings. Lithgow was twice sent to Bath at the royal expense, and maintained by the King for six months, until he had largely recovered his original health and strength, although his left arm remained incurably crushed.

Soon after his return to England, Lithgow was carried, by the King's direction to the residence of Gondomar, the Spanish ambassador at the English court, for the purpose of endeavouring to procure some redress of his grievances. Lithgow, finding the case he argued not likely to succeed, accused the Spaniard, before a crowd of courtiers, of deceit and ungentleman–like conduct. This charge he followed up with an act of violence on the person of the ambassador, for which, though his spirited conduct was much applauded, he was sent to the Marshalsea prison in Southwark, where he was confined for nine weeks.

Lithgow after this made several further attempts to procure some sort of redress or compensation. He petitioned the House of Commons, by a bill of grievances, but none of these attempts were successful. The last effort of this kind which he made was in 1626.

In 1627 he returned to Scotland; and still under the influence of that spirit which had urged him to roam through the world for so many years, he undertook a tour through the western isles. He was certainly on the island of Arran in the year 1628; but from this period on little more is known about him. It seems likely that soon after this he returned to Lanark, his native parish, where he remained till his death, some time between 1645 and 1650.

Lithgow made claim that in all his wanderings he had walked 36000 miles. His account of his travels is contained in his book: *Rare Adventures and Painful Peregrinations* (The Folio Society, 1974).

NINETEENTH AND EARLY TWENTIETH CENTURY MALAGA – IMPRESSIONS OF BRITISH AND AMERICAN VISITORS

Richard Ford (1796–1858) – Handbook for Travellers in Spain (1845)

Ford begins his description of Malaga by recommending accommodation. He notes that at both:

"... the hotel Alameda .... kept by Mr Hodson ... and the Victoria ... recently erected [nearby] and managed by Mr Frank, English comforts may be enjoyed under the Andalucian climate."

Moreover, readers are advised:

"Mr Hodson keeps a store near his hotel, where British beer, soda water etc may be had."

Amongst other inns, Ford offers the following choice:

"Fonda de los Tres Reyes ..... good and clean, [and] Parador de las Diligencias, dirty."

Ford then recommends the health benefits of the Malaga climate:

"Invalids, and especially those whose lungs are affected, will find the climate of Malaga superior to anything in Italy or Spain. The characteristics are constant sunshine and dryness of the air; in 1850 only seven days of real wet occurred; clear sunshine is the rule..... Winter, in our acceptation of the thing, here is almost unknown."

Referring to the city's river – the Gudalmedina – Ford writes that it is:

" a mere brook in summer, but a devastating torrent in winter. It is the bane and antidote of the city: the deposits block up the harbour, while ...it cleanses away with its freshes the accumulations of plague–engendering filth to which the inhabitants are strangely indifferent."

And Ford notes the shifting sea–water's edge:

"The sea meantime recedes; thus the old Moorish quay is now in the town, and the Alameda was covered with water last century."

Overall, the site of Malaga is a good one. Ford comments:

"Phoenician Malaga, like Cadiz, is of immemorial antiquity, and the judgment shown in the selection of the site is evidenced by a commercial existence and prosperity of 3000 years."

But although Ford found Malaga generally agreeable, he was of the view that at that time a short visit only was necessary:

"Malaga, being, as it was from its very beginning, a purely commercial city, and without arts or letters, is soon seen. Taste is here confined to raisins and sweet wine. A couple of days will more than suffice to the traveller."

But what there is to see is written about favourably.

"The panorama of sea and land is magnificent."

And he says of the Atarazana:

"The Moorish Atarazana, or dock–yard, is now in the town, from the sea's receding. A beautiful marble horse–shoe arch remains: this has been disfigured by a paltry shed, and narrowly escaped being pulled down in 1833; and there is now talk of the "necessity of new improvement. The Spaniard in authority has small feeling for Moorish art, which he considers a remnant of a barbarian infidel and invader; nay, he resents the admiration of foreigners, because it implies inferiority in himself."

And as regards the Alameda, he says it is:

"delicious: the houses on it are the best in Malaga; somewhat too sunny by day, the evening gas–lit promenade is most fashionable..... The walk is full of flowers and water."

Of the Fountain of Genoa (now in the Plaza de la Constitucion, but then in the Alameda) Ford refers critically to its:

"groups of female figures

somewhat undressed for Spanish propriety."

Ford mentions also the significant industry which at that time had quite recently grown up in Malaga.

"Iron–foundries, soap–fabrics and cotton–mills are fast rising. The chief impulse to all this [having been] given by the later energetic and enterprising Manuel Agustin de Heredia."

Nevertheless, to Ford:

"The tall smoking chimneys ... look odd under this azure sky, transported as it were from Lancashire, for their sooty sins."

And he expresses the fear that:

"the Malaguenans, whose true wealth lies in the produce of the sea and of the earth's surface, may waste their industry in pursuit of shadows. Wine and fruit are their real staples, not cotton bales and pigs of iron, the produce of Manchester and Birmingham. The ... mistake is to wish to make for themselves wares, bad and dear, in preference to importing them good and cheap."

Captain Charles Rochfort Scott – Excursions in the Mountains of Ronda and Granada (1838)

Writing in 1838 Captain Charles Rochfort Scott shared a sense experienced also by modern visitors as he approached the city:

"The appearance of Malaga on a near approach is mean and unprepossessing; nor is this an optical deception, for the suburbs are miserably poor and excessively dirty. This last, indeed, is a fault that the city may be charged with generally; and such is the contempt in which the virtue of cleanliness is held by the inhabitants. that, though the little river Guadalmedina winds its way through the heart of the city, requiring only to be properly husbanded to keep the place sweet and clean; yet, from mismanagement, it is itself suffered to become a nuisance; the scanty stream ... so obstructed by heaps of filth, brought out from the city, and thrown into its wide bed, that not having sufficient power to carry off the accumulated mass of corruption, it serves only (by keeping it constantly moist) to render the process of putrefaction more fetid and deadly."

However, on reaching the centre of the town a better impression is gained:

"The principal portion of the city is on the left bank of the Guadalmedina ('river of the city'). The change, on passing the bridge [over the Guadalmedina] is most agreeable; the first object that presents itself being the Alameda, a fine open space, lined on three sides with handsome houses, and on the fourth open to the refreshing westerly breezes. A shaded carriage drive goes round the quadrangle; and down its centre, a broad gravel walk, furnished with seats, and planted with flowers and shrubs, affords the public a delightful promenade. On a Sunday evening this Paseo is crowded with all classes of inhabitants; and the dark voluptuous Malaguena, as with mincing step she threads the motley throng, fails not to display her skill in fanning signals to her various acquaintances. The stranger, whilst following, with admiring eyes, the graceful movements of the fluttering parchment, little suspects that he is himself the subject of its telegraphic communications."

Referring to the Alcazaba, Scott comments:

"The Alcazaba ... has a better and more immediate command over the city and harbour than even the Gibralfaro itself. The walls of the [Alcazaba] were evidently constructed at the cost of some proud Roman temple, and were probably run up in great haste, as numerous fragments of columns, capitals etc are built in with the more suitable bricks which the Moors generally used when they bestowed pains upon their works.

The walls of the Alcazaba ... are studded with these venerable fragments, and are in a ... ruinous condition. The principal gateway is, however, tolerably perfect, and affords a fine specimen of Moorish architecture."

Turning his attention to the cathedral, Scott's view was that:

"it is a handsome building; but, from only one of its towers having been finished, its appearance is much injured. How frequently has it happened, and how much is it to be regretted, that edifices dedicated to the worship of the Deity, have, as in this instance, been planned and partly executed on a scale of magnificence totally disproportioned to the means possessed for completing them to the original design."

Indeed, Scott goes rather further:

"Besides the deformities that offend the eye in these patched up buildings ... a deplorable conviction is forced upon the mind, that these splendid piles were erected rather with a view to commemorate their founders than to promote the well-being of mankind; and that large sums of money have thus been vainly squandered, or, at best, lain profitless for ages; which might have been otherwise beneficially employed in the interests of Christianity."

Referring to the Aduana, Scott explains:

"Immediately under the Alcazaba stands an immense and rather handsome edifice, built not many years since as a custom-house; but, meeting with few customers in that line of business, it has recently been converted into a Royal cigar manufactory, and is now in a thriving condition [employing] 700 persons (women and children)".

Scott then returns to public health issues:

"The population of Malaga is estimated at sixty thousand souls. It was formerly much greater, and not many years since, considerably less, having been reduced from 80,000 to 40,000, by repeated visitations of the yellow fever, about the commencement of the present century."

In Scott's day:

"the greater proportion of the inhabitants [were] employed in the ... occupation of preparing wines and dried fruits for the foreign markets. Upwards of 18,000 butts of wine, sweet and dry, are annually shipped from Malaga, of which the chief part is taken by the Americans; but a vast quantity of the latter [ie the dry wine], under the name of Malaga Sherry, finds its way also into the cellars of ... England; whence, after undergoing a simple metonymical process, it flows down the public throat under its new name of 'old brown' or 'curiously old dry sherry'."

The Rev. John Alonzo Clark – Glimpses of the Old World – Vol II (1840)

Having taken a steamer from Gibraltar, Clark – a protestant cleric from Philadephia – describes his first impressions of Malaga thus:

"The town, lying under the shelter of lofty ranges of hills ... presented at first view, quite a picturesque appearance...."

However:

"The streets are very narrow, and contain such deposits of filth as no one can conceive who has not visited a Spanish town. The houses here – as they generally are in Spain – are built like castles, having an open court in the centre; the entrance to which, through immense and thick battened doors, is closely barred at night. The floors to their houses are made of stone or brick. The family usually live above – sometimes in the second or third story – the first, or basement story, being used for a stable....

So far, so good: but the Reverend Clark was easily moved to anger and disapproval. He writes:

"I ... spent a sabbath [in Malaga]. I never before witnessed such an entire desecration of the day of sacred rest. It seemed to me, that amongst the vast crowds that peopled this place, there were none that feared God, or regarded his institutions. All the shops and stores seemed to be open as on any other day. The markets and the Alameda were filled with men and women engaged in occupations of business or amusement; ships were unloading their freight, and open warehouses receiving it; merchants were in their counting rooms transacting their business – as though God has not said "Remember the sabbath day, and keep it holy". Bills were posted announcing that the theatre would be open .... The idle and dissipated were lounging around the streets, crowding the wharves, or sitting at the door of some cafe playing cards. All places seemed to be full of activity and life, but the lonely and desolate temples of the Lord."

Clark failed to find a Protestant church and so visited some which were Catholic. This provided him little cheer:

"I went to one of the Catholic parish churches .... The edifice was beautiful, being richly ornamented with gilded ceilings, fine paintings and statuary. The people, however, assembled there, were fed with husks – with an empty pantomime of crossings and ringing of bells, and bearing aloft of burning tapers at midday, of prostrations before images, and endless genuflexions. Mass was said or sung in a language which the people did not understand. There was no living voice of instruction, to guide the erring sinners to the cross – no intelligible form of sound words, to lift the hearts of the assembled worshippers in devout adoration to the Lord. I was sickened by the scene. I turned from the gaudy–decked priest and his assistants to examine the congregation. There was scarcely a well–dressed man among the number, and I

should think from their attire, but a very few ladies belonging to the more cultivated classes of society. The mass of the congregation consisted of beggars, attracted here by the hopes of obtaining alms, and of quite the lower class of people..... I have been informed from an intelligent source, that one reason of this desertion of the churches in Spain, is that the more cultivated classes of people have become disgusted with empty forms of popery, and the licentious and immoral lives of many of those who minister at the altar...."

Calming down a little, Clark describes the cathedral:

"The cathedral is the great charm of Malaga. I should have gone there on Sunday morning, but the services were held at a very early hour.... The exterior of this magnificent edifice is in an unfinished state ... but even in its present state it is very imposing. The interior is beautifully finished. The floor is a pavement of marble; every square slab being alternately white and brown. Four rows of immense columns or pilasters, thirty–two in all, run through the whole length of this building supporting the roof .... The high altar and the pulpit are encrusted with fine marble, and the choir ornamented in a style of peculiar elegance.... "

Clark was much impressed by this, the first great cathedral he had seen:

" I looked around in astonishment, ... my mind was impressed with unutterable ideas of vastness and sublimity.... The effect of this magnificent structure ... was to fill my mind with the deepest emotions of solemnity and awe, and to lift my thoughts ... I walked through its vast length and breadth, and found my feelings peculiarly attuned to devotion. Truly my heart mounted up to God."

But Clark was not one to remain relaxed for long. He soon noted that there were rather few worshippers in the cathedral, and

fulminated:

> *"There were but twenty persons present in the whole cathedral, with the exception of the sacerdotal band of performers in the choir. The exercises were not calculated to instruct, as the psalms chanted were in Latin, a the persons present seemed to view them in no other light tha as a sort of Sunday afternoon treat of fine music.*
>
> *I turned away, and paced the dusky aisles of this magnificent cathedral in bitterness of spirit, at the thought of the inadequate means afforded by the Roman Catholic church for the guidance of immortal spirits in the way everlasting.... What armies of priests this church has, that pass a lazy existence, saying over daily a few Latin prayers – singing their matins and vespers, and spending the rest of the time in eating and drinking, in sleep and indolence, while millions under their care are perishing for lack of knowledge, because they never heard the simple truth ...."*

Perhaps Clark chose badly to visit catholic southern Europe?

Overall, however, he seems to have been a genial person. Witness the following:

> *"Upon my first arrival ... I took up ... lodgings at an inn, the master of which spoke perfect English. An incident of rather an amusing character occurred here during the progress of my acquaintance with the landlord and his worthy dame. She was a widow when she married Mr S ..., and had had two children by a previous marriage. The daughter resided with them, and the son had gone to sea. I do not know that I have said anything to you about the cabin–boy that we had on board our passage across the Atlantic. He was uncommonly smart and sprightly. He was always singing or whistling, and apparently in the happiest mood, although every one, from the captain to the cook, seemed to think that he had an undoubted right to swear and scold him*

continually. All their anger and their oaths, however, seemed to make no impression upon this ... ...i.ht, who skipped

GW00383974

the least abuse ... ... spirits. I had not long been at my lodgings at Malaga, before I discovered that our landlady was the mother of Antonio. As soon as she learned I came out on board the Pennsylvania, her mouth was filled with inquiries about her sailor–boy. As she could speak nothing but Spanish, Mr S ..., her husband, the master of the house, had to act as her interpreter. I gave her all the information in my power in relation to her son. As she talked on of her child, the tears gushed from her eyes, and fell plentifully upon her cheek. I thought human nature and the mother's heart the same every where. I felt refreshed in witnessing this burst of natural affection. I asked her, as I was about to return to Gibraltar, what message I should carry to her son. She replied in Spanish, with all the fullness of a mother's heart, and in the simplicity of overflowing maternal affection, "Kiss him for me, and give him my best love." I delivered the message, but forebore the requested greeting ...."

William Cullen Bryant – Letters of a Traveller (1857)

> *"Our steamer was a propeller, and easily affected by the motion of the sea. It was a great relief to find ourselves, towards morning, in smoother water; and when the sun rose upon us, it was the genial and golden sun of Malaga.*
>
> *They have a way of making strangers who land at Malaga pay an exorbitant tax on their*

luggage; a fixed rate is exacted for every separate package, great or small, taken from the steamer to the wharf; another for its conveyance to the custom–house, and a certain tribute on every thing brought into the custom–house; and a separate charge on every object conveyed from the custom–house to the hotel. I heard of an American gentleman who, in this way, by some ingenious construction of the regulations in force, was made to pay twenty dollars; and then the rogue who had practised this imposition, told him that if he would do him the honor of employing him when he should leave the port, he would put his baggage on board of any steamer for a fifth part of the money.

In the Fonda de la Alameda, one of the best hotels in Spain, we took rooms looking upon the principal public walk of the city – a broad space, planted with rows of trees, mostly elms, which had not yet, on the first of December, parted with their leaves. The sun shone pleasantly into our windows for nearly the whole day, and we felt no need of artificial warmth. The fine weather tempted us out to look at the town, which resembles others in the south of Spain in the narrowness and crookedness of its streets; the same labyrinth of ways, no doubt, which was trodden by the inhabitants ages since, when they wore turbans. It is proverbially said in Malaga, that a priest cannot turn round in them without knocking off his hat. Many of them have a short stone pillar placed at each end in the middle of the passage, to prevent carriages from attempting to enter. The little dark shops on each side are scarcely larger than the narrow and shallow recesses in which the traders of Cairo and other towns in the East sit squatted among their merchandise; but the dwelling– houses, when the open street doors allowed us a peep at the courts within, had a pleasanter aspect. Here was an open square paved with black and white pebbles, in a sort of mosaic, representing foliage and flowers, and surrounded by a gallery resting on light stone columns with round arches. In the midst, generally, flowed a little fountain, and the place was made cheerful by orange trees and other ornamental evergreens, or by pots of flowers.

Our walk took us by two or three fruit markets, in which lay piles of oranges on mats, with lemons scarcely turned yellow, and baskets of pomegranates and medlars, but no grapes. "At this season you must not look for fresh grapes in Malaga," said one to whom I expressed my surprise; " however abundant they may be in Cartagena or Alicante. The wines we send abroad bear so high a price at the present time, that all our grapes go to the wine-press, and after the vintage there is not one to be seen."

Henry Havelock Ellis – The Soul of Spain (1908)

"Malaga is still, as it has been from the time of the Phoenicians, a very important commercial and industrial centre; it has an almost supremely fine climatic position, with the hottest and perhaps the most perfect winter weather of Continental Europe. Its people possess … a not uninteresting city, and they reveal a certain aspiration for urban development; but that executive ability, so marked in the Catalans, is here lacking. The languor of their climate seems always to affect the accomplishment of the Malaga people's great designs. Alike under Moorish rule and under Christian rule few great personalities have come out of Malaga, for at Malaga it is so easy to recline under the blue sky, amid the almost tropical vegetation, and therewith to be content."